Planning for the Unexpected:
Land-Use Development and Risk

LAURIE JOHNSON, AICP, SUZANNE FREW, AND LAURA SAMANT

TABLE OF CONTENTS

Preface	i
Chapter 1. Assessing Risk in Land-Use Planning	**1**
Defining Risk	3
Risk Types	3
Other Risk Characteristics	6
Risk and Land-Use Decisions	8
Chapter 2. A Risk Management Framework	**11**
What is Risk Management	12
How Risk is Managed	13
Chapter 3. Examining Four Programs to Manage Risks	**31**
Disaster-Resistant Berkeley:	
Uniting Disaster Management with Planning in California	32
Palm Beach County:	
The Front Lines for Florida's Ongoing Growth Management Efforts	35
Calvert County, Maryland:	
Reacting to Smart Growth Incentives	39
Saint Paul, Minnesota:	
Regional Tax-Base Sharing	42
Chapter 4. Putting It All Together: Establishing a Risk-Management-Based Approach to Planning in Your Community	**47**
Why Local Implementation is Best	48
Using the Land-Use Planning Framework for Implementation	49
Planners Are Ideally Situated to Do Risk Management	50
Planners Also Need to Seek Collaboration and Support	50
Growing Awareness of Risk-Based Planning	52
Appendix A. List of References and Bibliography	**55**

Acknowledgments

This report evolved out of the "Dealing with Public Risks Involved in Land Use Planning" Symposium, organized by the Public Entity Risk Institute in June 2001. Gary Binger, PERI Board of Directors and Director of the California Smart Growth Initiative of the Urban Land Institute, advocated for the PERI/APA collaboration to pursue and fund the project and continued as a committed supporter and coach.

Preparation of this report benefited from the contribution and support from many people and organizations—particularly through the tough times of intellectual challenge and world events following the terrorist attacks of 9/11. PERI provided the major financial support; PERI staff members, particularly Claire Reiss and Gerry Hoetmer, enthusiastically supported this project; founding PERI Board of Director, Felix Kloman, mentored the project team with his wealth of knowledge in public risk management; Jim Hecimovich, Jim Schwab, and Rhonda Smith, the editors for this report, provided valuable support and assistance; and Risk Management Solutions donated graphics and time to complete this manuscript.

More than 100 city and county staff members responded to the 2001 survey of local risk assessment and risk management practices. Management/staff members of Rio Blanco, Colorado; Bozeman, Montana; San Luis Obispo County, California; Bedford, Virginia; Irving, Texas; Ardmore, Oklahoma; East Greenwich, Rhode Island; and Windsor, Connecticut willingly shared local plans and processes in response to our survey. Isaac Hoyos, Palm Beach County, Florida; Randi Vogt, Calvert County, Maryland; Arrietta Chakos, City of Berkeley, California; and Matt Smith, City of St. Paul, Minnesota, generously reviewed and provided guidance on our case studies. Other professionals consulted in our research included: Diana McClure, Institute of Building and Home Safety; Andre LeDuc, Oregon showcase state; Kent Lim, U.S. Economic Development Administration; Bruce Baird, consultant; Tom Tobin, consultant; Rae Zimmermann, NYU; Bob Olsen, consultant; Rich Bernkof, U.S. Geological Survey; and many others.

But above all these, it was the efforts of Suzanne Frew and Laura Samant, assisting Laurie Johnson that made this report possible. Suzanne Frew bravely jumped off into the unknown and laid the initial foundation for the research. Laura Samant then took up the challenge when Suzanne returned from Russia with her newly adopted daughter, Christina. Laurie, Suzanne, and Laura now celebrate Laura's new daughter, Sophia. Together, they dedicate this work to Christina and Sophia. May they grow up in a world more prepared for risks—those understood and those we still struggle to understand.

Preface

Never before have planners in the U.S. been so sensitized to the possibility that catastrophic, unforeseen events can befall those who live and work in our communities. Sometimes even the unthinkable becomes reality. As millions of people watched the World Trade Center towers collapse, our illusions of safety from terrorism ended. Within a matter of minutes, it became clear the planning profession's best-made plans lay vulnerable to shifting world events and external influences never before imagined. We understand local plans and planning practices must be strengthened to combat a whole host of risks— both tangible and intangible, likely and unlikely. But exactly how do we do this?

While events that affect the well being of our communities often cannot be controlled, there are ways to better plan for them. Handling the unforeseen and the unexpected is what risk management is all about. Risk management is both a profession and a disciplinary practice for dealing with complicated systems and decisionmaking. Risk analysis techniques have been around for decades, especially in engineering fields where the behavior of systems can be modeled according to physical and chemical laws. More recently, the business world (particularly the insurance industry) has also developed its own practices that draw upon risk *management* methods for financial management.

For local governments, explicit risk management practices are more commonly applied in liability insurance purchases, risk pool participation, and management of public building and infrastructure assets. Many communities also have well-established environmental and fiscal impact assessment procedures, but these do not consider all the risks involved in each land-use decision. Surprisingly, with each land-use decision, a great deal of risk is retained unintentionally, simply because it is not identified. As a consequence, the feasibility of various decision options is rarely explored.

This report looks at the principles and practices of risk management and how these can be applied in land-use planning and development practices and protocols. When properly incorporated into land-use policies and development review processes, a risk-based framework will challenge community decision-makers to more fully consider the range of potential consequences as well as the alternatives for avoiding, reducing, or controlling them. Many of the illustrative examples and case studies draw heavily upon the authors' experience in natural hazards and financial risk management, as well as local government planning practices in California. Our case studies, in particular, explore how four communities have addressed and managed certain risks, the collaborative processes they undertook in doing so, and the outcomes and lessons learned.

As professionals, and as members of our own communities, we must renew our efforts to meet both well-known and newly emerging risks. With creativity, we have the tools, partners, support, and opportunities available to implement the processes described in the following pages. In doing so, we will be doing our part to create more robust, enjoyable, and secure communities for years to come.

Laurie A. Johnson, AICP; Laura Dwelley Samant; and Suzanne Frew

CHAPTER 1

Assessing Risk in Land-Use Planning

Governments have the most to learn about risk. Without a better grasp of the costs and benefits of the rules they create to control it, they can do more harm than good.
—JOHN SMUTNIAK
The Economist, January 24, 2004

On September 11, 2001, the extensive risks associated with one decades-old land-use decision for 16 acres of prime urban area became fatally evident. When the World Trade Center towers collapsed, thousands died, 13 million square feet of offices were destroyed, another 17 million square feet was damaged, more than 100,000 jobs were directly eliminated, and billions of dollars worth of assets were lost (City of New York 2001). The total economic price tag for the September 11 attacks is estimated at more than $120 billion (OECD 2003). As Figure 1-1 illustrates, the direct physical impacts of the World Trade Center disaster extended well beyond its 16-acre site. Suffering, economic and social losses, and fear spread throughout the region, nation, and world.

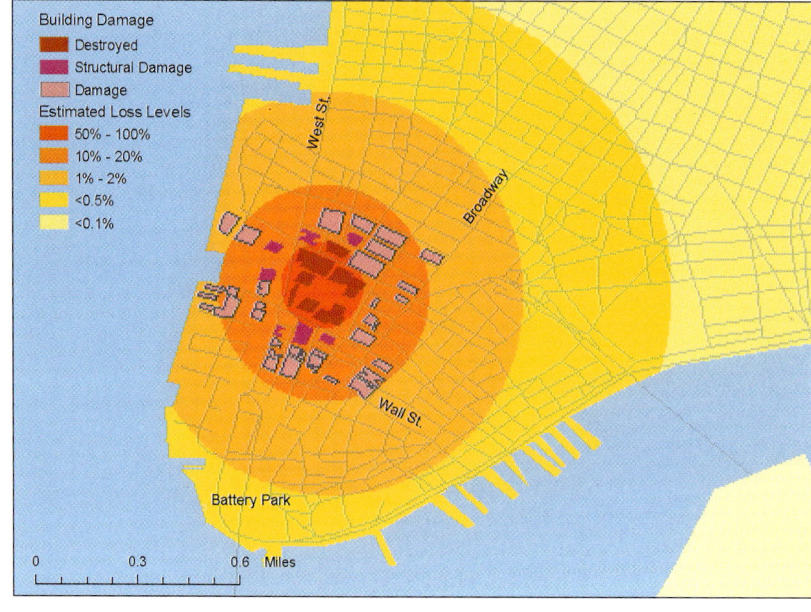

Figure 1-1. Building Damage and Loss in Lower Manhattan

Source: Image courtesy of Risk Management Solutions, Inc., © 2001.

The terrorist attacks on New York City and Washington, D.C., have had a profound impact on our sense of security and perceptions of social and economic vulnerability, and should also affect our approaches to land use.

Some of these impacts were unpredictable; others went hand-in-hand with urban life. The density of people and capital in modern urban high-rise development has inherent risks: any event that destroys a major building, such as a fire, a structural failure, or a terrorist attack, will have immense consequences. We can all debate whether the risks associated with skyscrapers and urban density outweigh their benefits. A series of land-use decisions made in the 1970s and 1980s, however, did result in many transportation, utility, communication, and emergency service networks being routed through or near the World Trade Center site. These land-use decisions concentrated regional risk and extended the impacts of this catastrophic event.

In addition to the destruction of the towers, portions of three subway lines were destroyed or disabled, disrupting for many months the essential transportation links that had served thousands of commuters. Two electrical substations were heavily damaged, and one of the two major north-south water lines traversing Manhattan was cut, leaving lower Manhattan vulnerable to power and water outages for weeks. Phone service was disrupted for lower Manhattan for weeks. Major radio and television antennae, formerly perched on top of the towers, disappeared in the rubble, interrupting media service when demand for news was at its highest. The main city emergency response office was located on the 23rd floor of the 7 World Trade Center building, along with computer databases critical for rebuilding activities, and was entirely destroyed when the structure collapsed on the afternoon of September 11. Even for crowded New York City, this concentration of critical facilities and essential services was unusual.

The terrorist attacks on New York City and Washington, D.C., have had a profound impact on our sense of security and perceptions of social and economic vulnerability, and should also affect our approaches to land use. Similar to the situation at the World Trade Center site, most communities unintentionally assume a great deal of risk as they develop. This can range from growing economic burdens when cities take on maintenance expenses for privately constructed infrastructure to rising flood damages as increasing percentages of paved surfaces funnel more water into local rivers.

Generally, the variety of options available to communities to manage or reduce risk is never explored. These unaddressed risks are then passed on to community residents, businesses, or government when, perhaps, they could have been easily eliminated or reduced if properly identified. In the coming decades, our communities will continue to grow more complex and vulnerable as the country's population expands and globalization and technology continue to dramatically change our lifestyles. While local governments and residents will absorb many new risks, an increasing number of techniques are available to address this problem.

Risk management is a discipline that has been used by engineers, insurance companies, and corporate risk managers for decades. Its principles and practices can be applied to local land-use decision making. As our communities grow ever more complex, planners can use these techniques to help ensure that their communities are as resilient as possible by thoughtfully addressing risks in development plans and development review, and also considering the long-term consequences of risk on the entire community.

DEFINING RISK

To understand risk management and how it relates to local planning functions, we must first understand what *risk* is. Risk definitions are as diverse as the range of risks they describe. As planners, we frequently deal with different risk characterizations. For national- and state-level environmental review, there is a checklist of risks describing various potential negative effects with a focus on environmental concerns. In the natural hazards field, risk is the result of a hazard phenomenon (e.g., a flood, hurricane, or earthquake) and its interaction with the elements within the community—people, buildings, economic activity, and infrastructure—vulnerable to such an impact. City managers often use the term *risk* to refer to liability concerns, workers compensation, employee relations, and to a lesser extent, public property management.

In an effort to standardize the definition for the field of risk management, the International Organization for Standardization (ISO) recently identified risk as the "combination of the chance of an event and its consequences" (ISO 2002). This is a broad definition applicable to many disciplines. In other words, risk varies both with the impacts of a potential undesirable event and the likeliness of that event to occur.

If we were to write out the definition of risk as an illustrative formula, it would look something like:

$$\text{Hazard} \times \text{Exposure} \times \text{Vulnerability} = \text{Risk}$$

Where,

> *Hazard* is the natural phenomenon or triggering event that has both a *size* and *frequency* linked to its probability of occurrence. *Size* or *severity* describes how large the impacts of the event might be. *Frequency* describes how often it might happen.
>
> *Exposure* refers to the elements within the community (people, buildings, economic activity, and infrastructure) that can experience the hazard.
>
> *Vulnerability* is the function that relates how likely each exposed community element is to be damaged if a hazard event occurs.
>
> *Risk* is the outcome or consequence of the interaction between these three variables—when a hazard effects vulnerable elements in a community.

RISK TYPES

Risks can be categorized in numerous ways. Table 1-1 illustrates the five risk categories we will refer to regularly: capital stock, environmental, economic, social and cultural, and institutional and policy. Many are expressed as loss types, which can be further subdivided into direct, indirect, and

As our communities grow ever more complex, planners can use risk management techniques to help ensure that their communities are as resilient as possible....

Table 1-1.
Examples of Five Risk Categories

1. Capital Stock Risks
- Damage to government buildings
- Damage to essential facilities
- Damage to residences
- Damage to lifelines/utilities
- Damage to transportation systems
- Damage to machinery or equipment
- Damage to furnishings
- Loss of inventory
- Damage to crops
- Loss of function of facilities

2. Environmental Risks
- Water pollution
- Air pollution
- Loss of biodiversity
- Disruption of wildlife
- Noise pollution
- Light pollution
- Loss of natural beauty

3. Economic Risks
- Financial loss to government
- Financial loss to business
- Financial loss to residents
- Reduced tax income
- Reduced business income
- Increased government expenditures
- Lack of affordable housing
- Loss of high-paying jobs

4. Social and Cultural Risks
- Loss of life/injury/illness
- Loss of residence
- Loss of cultural/historical resources
- Loss of quality of life
- Demographic change
- Impacts on vulnerable populations
- Change in neighborhood character

5. Instutional and Policy Risks
- Liability
- Damage to reputation
- Staff turnover
- Erosion of vision and goals
- Increased distrust of government
- Undermining of other policies

intangible losses (Handmer and Thompson 1996). Direct damages are often physical and quantifiable. Indirect losses are generally a consequence of direct damage that can be financially quantified. Intangible or nonmarket losses describe impacts for which there is no commonly agreed method of evaluation. They include death and illness, reputation impacts, and quality-of-life changes. Some of these are familiar considerations in land-use practices; others are less tangible issue areas for planners but still affect planning goals in significant ways. Some also cascade across jurisdictional boundaries (political and geographic), often limiting our understanding and actual quantification of the risk effects.

Capital Stock Risks

Capital stock is the physical composition of a community. It includes the public and private lands, buildings, essential facilities (such as hospitals, police and fire stations, schools, dams, and power plants), and infrastructure (such as the physical conveyances of power, water, sewer, gas, telephones, and other communications services, as well as streets, highways, ports, airports, and railroads). Risks to capital stock include the:

- potential for damage to buildings, their contents, or to equipment;
- possibility of infrastructure damage or service outages; and
- potential loss of functionality due to a physical disruption or service outages.

The enforcement of subdivision standards and building and utility codes are common steps taken during the land development process to reduce capital stock risks.

Environmental Risks

The environment includes the natural habitat (such as wetlands and forests), biological resources, air and water resources, and urban landscapes. Environmental risks come from natural and man-made hazards; impacts on biodiversity, wildlife habitat, and migration routes; and air and water pollution. Within urban areas, environmental risks can also emerge from impacts on urban form and aesthetics, such as building mass and density, noise, signage, lighting, and cityscapes. Many public policies and procedures have evolved to address these development risks. They include environmental impact analyses, architectural design guidelines and review processes, hazard mapping and setback requirements, and site development ordinances.

Economic Risks

The economy is the lifeline of a community and drives long-term sustainability. The local business community, private and public revenue streams, jobs, land values, and the public tax base all play a role in a community's economy. Economic risks associated with land development include:

- neighborhood and regional economic changes, both short and long term;
- downshifts in jobs, revenue (i.e., retail sales, real estate transactions, etc.), and market share; and
- variations in the business community's composition and effectiveness.

Fiscal impact analyses are often undertaken to help identify potential economic risks associated with development. Economic impact analyses are also used to understand future risks and trends, such as the state of the local economy and external trends and forces.

Social and Cultural Risks

The social and cultural structure of a community includes its residents, cultural and historical identity and organization, and its community services. The primary social risks communities consider in development review involve the potential for injury and loss of life. Other social risks that may result from land development are neighborhood and regional demographic changes; impacts on vulnerable, and often marginalized, populations, including the elderly, disabled, immigrant and/or non-English speaking groups, single-parent households, women and children, and the poor; neighborhood degradation; crime and other safety-related issues; and changes in historic or cultural character. Quality of life for the full range of community members has gained increasing prominence as a critical element of community social and economic sustainability. Often, the social risks posed by a development project are not readily identifiable during the review process and only evolve over the months or years that follow. New development can stimulate neighborhood revitalization, for example, but may also reduce affordable housing, forcing the poor into overcrowded living conditions or out of the neighborhood altogether.

The social and cultural structure of a community includes its residents, cultural and historical identity and organization, and its community services.

Institutional and Policy Risks

Public agencies accept new levels and conditions of risk with every development policy or approval decision. Often these are the hidden costs of land development and the burden government accepts as part of its functional responsibilities. Liability introduced through development activities is a growing risk for institutions. In addition, for every project, public services, such as police and fire, waste disposal, street and drainage systems, and utility systems, must be extended and maintained. Over time, the costs of services and maintenance may surpass the benefits a development project initially provides, and the cumulative effects of multiple projects can far exceed the burden accepted with each individual project approval. Long-term social and economic liabilities, such as staff turnover or increased distrust of government, can be introduced as a result. *Reputation risk* is often overlooked but can be created with unpopular land-use policies or changing community character. *Policy risk* is also inherent in each land-use decision. The conditions of development approval or denial can instigate organizational and political changes, such as undermining other policies or erosion of a policy base.

OTHER RISK CHARACTERISTICS

Regardless of the type, risk is dynamic, changing with location, time, perspective, and conditions. The extent and severity of a particular risk can vary from one location—a parcel area, neighborhood, city, region, or state—to another. This is easily illustrated through earthquake shaking, which is strongest near the fault where an earthquake occurs and weakens as you move further away. Shaking can also be affected by geologic conditions, such as a pocket of soft soils distant from a fault but with characteristics that, nonetheless, amplify shaking to higher levels. Similarly, the risks associated with a particular project, such as a residential subdivision or a commercial shopping center, vary with that project's location. In an environmentally sensitive area, there may be risk the development could damage air quality, ecosystems, or natural beauty. Move the same project to another location, and development occupants could be exposed to risk, such as noise pollution or exposure to hazardous materials.

The same event may also pose different risks to different groups in a community—the unique "communities with a community" often emerging out of business, geographical, or political relationships, or sociocultural ties (e.g., language, ethnicity, or family structure), which continually develop and change. Some events can affect only commercial ventures, while others affect only homeowners or low-income renters. Local government may directly bear the brunt of some risks, such as damage to buildings or infrastructure they own or a reduction in public revenue streams. They also indirectly bear other risks with an impact on the status quo of a community, such as the loss of affordable housing. Who a risk affects directly can determine who can manage that risk as well as who is motivated to manage it.

Risk Concentrations

A community with all its major hospitals in one area becomes especially vulnerable to any event isolating that area from other parts of the community, such as a natural disaster or major traffic accidents. Concentrations of economic risks often occur in communities overly dependent upon one industry for employment or critical programs with one variable source of revenue, such as sales tax. Social risks can be concentrated when one vulnerable segment of the population could be disproportionately affected by a single event. For example, low-income residents in some California communities live primarily in 1960s-era buildings with "soft" first stories, a structural feature that makes buildings particularly vulnerable to earthquakes. Any earthquake in these communities is likely to cause significantly more hardship to low-income residents than to other segments of the population.

The implosion of the San Francisco Bay Area's dot-com industry provides a striking example of economic risk concentration and the impact the new global economy can have on land use. Known as the mecca of the dot-com miracle, the Bay Area was infused with extensive development and redevelopment in the late 1990s and the first few years of the 2000s. The resulting change was quite prominent in San Francisco's (formerly run-down) warehouse district known as the South of Market Area (SOMA). Longstanding local businesses, artists, and home and business renters were forced to relocate as real estate prices soared. Land-use battles dominated local elections and, within a few years, the economic and cultural vitality of the SOMA District (and much of the Bay Area) was radically transformed.

As dramatically as dot-com mania exploded onto the scene, its collapse proved equally as staggering. Bankruptcy notices replaced the endless job listings in local and national newspapers. Newly renovated buildings, carefully constructed to appeal to the new, young urbanite, closed their doors. One after another, new businesses folded. Local support industries, such as restaurants, dry cleaners, and entertainment centers, collapsed as residents lost their jobs and investments. The dot-com boom and bust demonstrated the complexity of economic cycles on community fragility. It raised new questions in communities on how best to attract and support new ideas and technologies, and it exposed deep vulnerabilities in our changing marketplace. These and other risks must be effectively addressed in order to avert catastrophic consequences for a community, its business stakeholders, and the sustainability of the local tax base.

Risk Variation

It is important to consider risks incurred by the complete lifecycle of any development project. Often, decisions made today do not fully account for changing conditions that occur five, 10, 20, or more years later. For example, while the meaningful "economic life" of buildings and infrastructure is often viewed in a 30-year timeframe (derived from mortgage terms), we generally expect the continued occupation and use of most structures beyond this timeframe. The costs of long-term maintenance and upgrades and the risk of functionality losses over time are rarely accounted for in initial decision making. Risk varies as development ages, communities grow more or less dense, residents grow richer or poorer, population demographics shift, issues of terrorism further affect civil society, and local practices change. Land-use patterns today, with homes built in formerly wild areas protected from burning for decades, may have a greater risk from wildfires than half a century ago. On the other hand, improved technology, such as better methods to store and dispose of hazardous materials, may reduce health risks from levels seen in previous generations.

While one single land-use decision may not increase risk significantly, years of small decisions that incrementally increase risk can lead to unacceptable risk levels.

Risk Accumulation

While one single land-use decision may not increase risk significantly, years of small decisions that incrementally increase risk can lead to unacceptable risk levels. A good example is the gradually increasing flood risk due to cumulative land-use decisions. Communities facing flood risk may have strong regulations limiting or preventing development in the floodplain. Few jurisdictions have recognized, however, that development in their entire community may contribute to the height of floodwaters. When it rains, water seeps into the ground and saturates soils, at which point it starts to run off into local streams and rivers. When soils are paved over by development, water can no longer soak easily into the ground; instead, it flows directly over land into river and stream basins, filling up rivers and basins more quickly. This is a particular problem for communities with small watersheds.

> **RIPPLE EFFECTS OF THE JULY 2001 BALTIMORE TRAIN DERAILMENT**
>
> A train accident on July 18, 2001, in a tunnel beneath downtown Baltimore further demonstrates risk dependencies on an even finer scale. Eleven cars of a CSX (60 cars and three locomotives) transportation freight train derailed. One damaged tanker railcar was transporting approximately 26,000 gallons of liquid tripoplylene. A fire erupted and burned for several days.
>
> Ripples of health, economic, and social consequences resulted from the accident. The heavy smoke and fumes drifted across downtown Baltimore, forcing the closure of all roads leading into the city. The July 18 and 19 Baltimore Orioles Baseball games at nearby Camden Yards Stadium were then cancelled. A water main burst, flooding local streets. Fiber-optic cables running through the tunnel and backup cables running alongside the tunnel were severed and destroyed by the fire, water, and wreckage. Internet services were disrupted across the northeastern U.S., and telephone service to western Maryland was also affected. "That tunnel is basically the I-95 of the East Coast for fiber," said John Grundey, president of LAI Construction Services, Inc. of White March, which built the fiber-optic line detour around the break. "It was a once-in-a-lifetime place for vulnerability."
>
> Source: FEMA 2003, 2-21.

One rapidly developing community, Charlotte, North Carolina, studied this problem after experiencing higher than expected flood levels for several years. They found that when the metro area is fully developed as planned, the height of the 100-year flood will be as much as 2.5 feet higher and encompass significantly more acres than when flood maps were originally drawn for the community. Clearly, the community faces an increasing risk directly linked to its development decisions. Charlotte is the rare community that has identified this risk and taken steps to manage it; most communities remain unaware of whether and how their land-use decisions affect future flood levels.

Risk Echoes

One consequence often causes another. For example, a power outage may cause a sewage spill leading to environmental damage. Rain that causes a flood can also trigger landslides. The World Trade Center disaster showed how specific land-use decisions (e.g., concentrating many items of key infrastructure through one node) caused significant secondary risks as lower Manhattan residents struggled to cope without power, water, phone, or transport after the disaster. The cascading effect of natural, technological, and human-caused hazards compounds both short- and long-term costs and losses. Many of the recent catastrophic disasters, such as the 1995 Kobe earthquake, illustrate the regional and even global nature of "cascading impacts." Earthquake damage at the Port of Kobe permanently altered container shipping patterns throughout Asia and substantially affected the City of Kobe's revenue base.

RISK AND LAND-USE DECISIONS

Risk can be introduced in many different forms in land-use decision making. Some risks are straightforward, such as the physical risks that accompany decisions allowing development in a floodplain. Clearly, development in that type of location places physical and economic assets and lives at risk. Other decisions increase risk in less obvious ways by concentrating risks, accumulating risks over time, exacerbating or ignoring emerging risks, or increasing some types of risks while reducing others. For example, there is an overarching risk that the goals and objectives for a particular land development project may not materialize, just as a portfolio of stocks may not perform at the desired level.

Some development decisions may reduce a certain set of risks but increase others. A much-discussed example of this type of risk is urban sprawl. While new development brings tax revenues, sprawling growth can also bring many negative effects, including increased costs to build and maintain infrastructure and schools, increased pollution as commuters travel further from jobs, and social dislocation and loss of sense of place as communities decentralize and lose individual character. By focusing only on income, communities ignore risks associated with expenditures, environmental health, and social cohesion. Other examples include construction of coastal structures that reduce erosion in one area but exacerbate it down the coastline and development of "terrorism-resistant" structures that have greater ability to withstand bomb blasts but can be aesthetically unappealing, decrease access to the structure, and alienate the public. These examples illustrate the importance of communities examining all types of risks a development decision brings.

Many of the risks introduced through land-use decisions are what we could term emerging risks. They are threats to the community that are newly recognized and linked to changes in the way communities are structured, to new technologies, or to scientific advances. Certainly, planners cannot prevent these types of risks from appearing in communities before they are recognized. We can, however, work to design planning processes that can adapt to respond to new risks as we learn about them.

The Current Practice of Risk Management in Land-Use Planning

Planners have an increasing variety of tools with which to identify and manage risks related to land use. Risk management options include: comprehensive or general plans, specific or area plans, zoning ordinances, subdivision regulations, building codes, capital improvement plans, budgets, environmental impact reports, and other common planning approaches. Many jurisdictions around the country currently use these methods to manage some aspects of their risk. Many others, however, do very little to examine common risks introduced by new development. Almost no jurisdictions have procedures that recognize the concentrated, cumulative, and multifaceted risks like those discussed above.

APA PAS survey result. To better understand the current practice of risk management in land-use decision making, a survey about local risk assessment and land development review procedures was mailed to the planning agencies, consultants, and educational institutions that subscribe to APA's Planning Advisory Service (PAS). It asked agencies to characterize their development review process, define how risk assessment is incorporated into this process, identify documents or procedures that provide a basis for the process, and discuss how staff and the public are involved in the process. More than 100 agencies responded from 35 different states, representing cities and counties of varying population sizes.

More than half of the communities who responded to the survey engage in some risk management activities during the development review process. Generally, procedures are focused on specific issues of local concern, most often environmental issues, such as water pollution or maintaining open space. About 75 percent of communities engage in risk management screen projects for environmental impacts. As regards screening for other risks, the results varied widely. Some communities focused on particular natural hazards (50 percent), consistency with jurisdiction policies (43 percent), economic development impacts (18 percent), or public safety concerns (14 percent). Fewer than 10 percent of communities with risk-screening procedures look for impacts on historic and cultural resources or public liability.

It is clear that the definition of risk used in this report is not standard among planning offices, particularly in the breadth of the phenomena it covers. In some communities, the term *risk management* suggests only issues associated with worker's compensation complaints, lawsuits, or emergency response planning. Very few communities (7 percent) screened for a comprehensive array of risks or complex, accumulating, or emerging risks.

Communities actively engaging in some sort of risk screening use a variety of different approaches. Risk-screening and management techniques cited included the following:

- Requiring developers to submit risk studies and proposed mitigation approaches when applying for permits

- Assessing fees to cover costs for in-house risk evaluations

- Conducting development review with multidepartmental committees (e.g. planning, building/engineering, health, fire, police) so that a broad range of concerns can be identified

We found that certain types of development applications (e.g. subdivision, annexation, land-use amendments, or rezoning requests) can trigger a screening for risk. For most responding agencies, the public is included in the development review processes when public hearings are conducted by local planning commissions. More than half (55 percent) of the responding agencies had developed their own processes or procedures while others based their procedures on the National Environmental Policy Act (NEPA), state environmental regulations, regulations from the Federal Emergency Management Association (FEMA), or other state and local ordinances.

Four-fifths of the responding agencies with risk programs had their procedures in place for more than five years, and more than a third had theirs in place for at least 20 years. Nearly all agencies with a risk assessment process either enacted the process voluntarily (47 percent) or in response to a state or federal mandate (42 percent). There was a strong correlation between agencies that had environmental risk assessment procedures in place and those with mandated procedures in place for at least 20 years. One possibility may be that NEPA and subsequent state environmental regulations have been catalysts for local adoption of risk assessment processes.

IBHS/APA survey results. "Are We Planning Safer Communities?", a study conducted in December 2001 by the Institute for Business and Home Safety (IBHS) and APA, asked 500 planners nationwide to consider whether their local plans are really making a difference in disaster prevention, particularly earthquake disaster prevention (Steinberg and Burby 2002). As part of the study, IBHS developed an eight-point rating system that considered the overall plan quality, data quality, community support, and specific policies, to name a few. The mean score for all communities was 48 percent, which is a B-minus on IBHS's safety report card, suggesting typical plans address about only half of the key elements contributing to a safe, hazard-resistant community (McClure 2002). The study also concluded, "communities making the greatest improvements in safety are located in states that require hazard elements in local plans" (Steinburg and Burby 2002).

Managing Risks

These survey findings suggest many communities are aware that land-use decisions can contribute to rising risk and are concerned enough to independently develop procedures to manage risk. They also indicate that state and federal mandates are effective at establishing local risk management programs, although whether mandated programs are more or less successful at reducing risks over time than locally initiated programs cannot be determined from these surveys. A concerning finding is that nearly half of all communities responding to the PAS survey have no consistently applied procedures to identify and manage even the most basic risks. Further, it is clear very few communities have a broad, flexible risk review process with the potential to identify and address the increasingly complex risks threatening communities.

It will never be possible to screen for all risks that communities face when new development and land-use decisions are made. This is largely because communities and risks are constantly changing. New threats are discovered every year. Many of the oldest and largest risks facing communities are too costly or technically impossible to eliminate. It is possible, however, to improve land development planning and review processes to better screen for risks, to reduce many of them to acceptable levels, and to control risks before they grow unmanageable. The next chapter explores the tools and techniques available to manage risks.

CHAPTER 2

A Risk Management Framework

The revolutionary idea that defines the boundary between modern times and the past is the mastery of risk: the notion that the future is more than a whim of the gods and that men and women are not passive before nature.
—Peter L. Bernstein
Against the Gods: The Remarkable Story of Risk

Only in the last few centuries did human beings discover that the future was not merely a mirror of the past. Modern societies have advanced beyond thinking that what happens is merely a result of luck, divine destiny, faith, or instinct. As industrialized societies evolved, individuals and businesses began adopting more logical, consistent, and disciplined ways for considering the future's uncertainties and avoiding unnecessary waste (Kloman 1999). Today, the discipline of risk management allows us to systematically make good decisions that anticipate probable future events.

WHAT IS RISK MANAGEMENT?

The term *risk management* is used to describe the process of identifying the potential impacts of events, such as natural disasters or development decisions, and formally applying policies, processes, and practices to address those impacts. It provides a structured approach to holistically evaluate the range of factors that facilitate or impede community welfare. It creates a common valuation system—generally financial—for quantifying, comparing, and making risk management decisions. And, most importantly, it provides a broader set of decision options for handling risks.

Risk management techniques emerged in the early twentieth century as responsibility for risk began to shift away from the individual to government and businesses. The adoption by states of workers' compensation laws and the implementation of social insurance schemes, such as pensions, represent important milestones in this shift. In 1921, economist Frank Knight, in his book, *Risk, Uncertainty, and Profit*, proposed risk was measurable and could be separated from uncertainty. It was around this time the field of risk management in the United States was born. The discipline of risk management matured in the 1950s and 1960s as engineers and professional insurance managers began quantifying the "cost of risks" in order to determine acceptable levels of risk in nuclear safety or to compare the price of insurance with alternative risk management strategies, such as self-funding and loss-control approaches.

Nobel Prize–winning economist and mathematician Harry Markowitz is credited with both the theoretical and practical innovations used by the financial and insurance industries for managing and selecting investments (Bernstein 1996). He described how probability theory could be used to assess both the risk and expected return on investments. It took the stock market crash of 1973–1974 to convince investors they should be interested in risk as well as return on their investment portfolios, and it took the major losses of Hurricane Andrew (1992) and the 1994 Northridge Earthquake to convince insurers they also needed to adopt better methods to select and manage their portfolios of insured properties (Bernstein 1996; EERI 1997). Shrinking local budgets and the rising costs of sprawl and security may be the instigating factors that convince public agencies to consider more holistic risk management approaches for the public portfolio of assets, including capital stock, residents, and quality of life.

For most public agencies, risk management functions are centered on institutional and capital-stock-related risks. The agendas of public risk management associations cover public property and liability insurance, workers' compensation, safety and loss prevention, loss control and claims management, and employee relations and benefits. A number of associations and institutes that gear a portion or all of their membership services and training toward public risk issues. Here are a few with their Web site addresses:

- The Public Entity Risk Institute (PERI) (*www.riskinstitute.org*)
- The Public Agency Risk Management Association (PARMA) (*www.parma.org*)
- The Public Risk Management Association (PRIMA) (*www.primacentral.com*)
- The Nonprofit Risk Management Center (NRMC) (*www.nonprofitrisk.org*)
- The Public Utilities Risk Management Association (PURMA) (*www.purma.org*)
- The Risk and Insurance Management Society (RIMS) (*www.rims.org*)

Public risk pools are common in most parts of the country and typically aid public entities in purchasing local liability insurance and other insurance products. In effect, these pools operate similarly to our health insurance schemes (HMOs, PPOs, and Medicare) by distributing the risks across a broader geographic base and consequently lowering premiums. Public agencies have taken increasing interest in financial stability, the tax base, and bond ratings, thereby anticipating risks to revenue streams (Reiss 2001).

Risk management practices are present in several key areas of planning as well. The environment has evolved as perhaps the single most focused area of review in planning today due to legal mandates for environmental review and protection enacted at the national level (and, in many cases, state level) in the 1970s and 1980s. Today's public and local leaders are questioning the type of growth occurring, how much it costs, who pays, and what the effects are on the environment, but they need to ensure that they are attentive to the many other effects growth has on a community's residents. A risk-based framework for land-use planning offers public agencies a rational means for managing inevitable change.

HOW RISK IS MANAGED

Risk management aims to anticipate and control the unforeseen and unexpected. A broad framework can be used to characterize and manage risks of diverse types. This framework has four major steps:

Step 1. Identifying risks
Step 2. Assessing and quantifying risks
Step 3. Making and implementing risk management decisions
Step 4. Monitoring and implementation over time

Each of these steps is discussed here in greater detail, and tools and techniques are also explored. Specific applications of these methods to land-use planning are provided wherever possible.

Step 1. Identifying Risks

The risk management process begins with identifying which risks have the potential to harm a community and, therefore, need to be assessed and managed. Risk identification can be project focused, or operational and event focused. For a particular project, such as development of a new subdivision, the goal may be to identify all of the events that could trigger adverse impacts to, or be caused by, the new development. Alternately, the community may wish to identify the range of potential impacts and unforeseen consequences that might occur as a result of a particular event, such as a hurricane or an economic slowdown. This process involves ascertaining potential risk-triggering events, also called hazards, that might occur in the area of interest and which community elements are exposed to these events.

For land development, this process is initiated in many communities with an environmental review. A number of states and communities have environmental disclosure laws, patterned after the National Environmental Policy Act (NEPA). These laws require that the potential environmental effects of both public and private projects be considered before any final action is taken on a project. In managing the process, agencies typically have a checklist of environmental conditions an applicant must meet. These checklists point out issues of environmental concern requiring further study or remediation measures. A similar approach can be taken for the many other types of risks that face communities.

Risk identification procedures should be flexible enough to call out cumulative, emerging, and secondary risks. Structured approaches, such as checklists and geographic data analyses, can be combined with brainstorming to identify risks that are not straightforward.

A risk-based framework for land-use planning offers public agencies a rational means for managing inevitable change.

Identifying triggering events. Each community will have a unique list of triggering events that are of concern, based on its geographic setting and social fabric. Table 2-1 lists some possible risk triggers, but there are many others that could be listed under each category, and additional categories could be created. A community-specific list of potential risk triggers can be constructed by studying historical events, discussing risk with specialists, and scanning available risk maps and studies.

Each risk trigger can be characterized by examining answers to the following questions:

- Where could the event occur? Is it limited to a specific geographic area?

- How often could the event occur? What is the probability of the event occurring at any given point in time?

- What size, strength, or magnitude is the event? Could it occur at different strengths with different frequencies? Could this event trigger any secondary events (e.g., a bomb blast could lead to a chemical spill; a downturn in local sales tax revenue could reduce funding for local wetlands protection programs)?

For some hazards, detailed responses to these questions will be readily available in numerical form. Others will need to be characterized qualitatively using descriptors such as *severe* or broad ranges such as *likely to occur at least once in 100 years* (e.g., a 100-year flood zone). Some potential triggers can only be partially characterized. For example, assigning probabilities to the occurrence of terrorist attacks is generally not possible; in many cases we can only say that such attacks are possible.

Each community will have a unique list of triggering events that are of concern, based on its geographic setting and social fabric.

Table 2-1.
Examples of Risk Triggering Events

Natural Hazards	Human-caused Hazards	Socioeconomic Disruption
Earthquake	Terrorist attack	Downturn of specific sector
Flood	Power outage	Jobs-housing imbalance
Wildfire	Hazardous gas release	Low-density development
Coastal erosion	Effluent spill	Population flight
Landslide	Crime	Population increase
Tornado	Cyber terrorism	Political change

Identifying vulnerable exposures. At a broad level, all of the buildings, their contents, infrastructure, people, and natural features in a community are exposed to some type of risk. As part of identifying risk, it is important to identify the portions of the jurisdiction of concern. For each element in a community, the features that determine risk include the following:

- The location of the item, particularly whether it is located in a geographic zone prone to a particular hazard or triggering event

- The physical properties of the element, including number of items, size, materials, construction quality, etc.

- The economic properties of the element, including the direct value of the item (e.g., the replacement cost of a building and its contents) and its indirect value (e.g., the number and economic value of jobs associated with the item, tax revenues generated, cost to replace functions of item)

- The social properties of the element, such as the number and characteristics of people who use the item at risk, and historical and cultural attributes

- The element's institutional and policy aspects, such as associated liability, impact on morale, or impact on community goals and vision

Again, some of this information may be available in numerical form, whereas other details by definition are subjective.

Tools to identify risks. A historical examination of risk, risk checklists, and geographic information systems (GIS) are all useful tools for a community trying to clearly assess its various types of risk.

- *Examining the history of risk* in your community or similar communities can provide insights into frequencies of different types of events and the elements most likely to be affected. Historical events provide only limited information for most types of hazards because past events may not represent the range of possible future events. Some hazards occur so rarely that few observations have been recorded in a particular location (e.g., volcanic eruptions) and others are emerging or changing with technology or society (e.g., Internet viruses). A useful analysis technique can be to assess what would happen if a historical occurrence, such as a wildfire, explosion, or power outage, reoccurred and affected the current infrastructure and population. Sometimes, a past event of minor consequence would produce significantly greater impact if it occurred in the larger, more complex communities of today. Useful resources include: historical archives and newspaper accounts, scientific and cultural reports, topographical maps, and environmental clues (e.g., erosion features, burn areas). For institutional risks, it is useful to examine the community's loss history, insurance payouts, budget shortfalls, and other public records.

- *Risk checklists* are an excellent tool for identifying risks and characterizing areas of concern difficult to quantify. Checklists are best used when they are focused on a particular area of risk (e.g., environmental risk) or the impact of a certain type of project on a wide range of risks (e.g., development of a subdivision). By taking the evaluator through a broad range of topics, checklists can bring to light the impact of activities not readily apparent, such as secondary risks triggered by a hazard. Checklists ensure that a systematic procedure is followed for all land-use decisions. (See the sidebar on the following page for an example.)

- *GIS* allows communities to track many different aspects of their infrastructure and population in map format and to overlay hazards with different elements of the community. GIS can be a powerful analysis tool, processing large amounts of data about development trends, geographic features, and a host of other issues. It can also be an effective presentation tool, creating maps that clearly show risks to lay audiences. Figure 2-1 illustrates how a triggering event can be overlaid on various data layers. GIS provides a powerful tool to apply a McHargian-style approach of overlaying many pieces of information about a community to identify zones appropriate for specific types of development. Outlined in his 1969 publication, *Design With Nature*, Ian McHarg showed how to identify environmentally sensitive areas and develop projects that minimize environmental impacts. The same concept of overlaying many pieces of scientific and social information to identify intersections and locations of maximum and minimum concern can be applied to many other risks of concern.

Risk checklists are an excellent tool for identifying risks and characterizing areas of concern difficult to quantify.

ENVIRONMENTAL RISK IDENTIFICATION IN CALIFORNIA

The California Environmental Quality Act (CEQA), passed in 1970, requires all public agencies to identify environmental impacts associated with a proposed project, and also provide feasible measures to mitigate any significant, adverse impacts of the project (*www.ceres.ca.gov*). CEQA applies to all large-scale discretionary projects at all levels of government, including approval of private development projects by state, regional, and local agencies. Discretionary projects include plan approvals and major project entitlements but do not include more routine ministerial projects, such as the issuance of building permits.

At the start of a development application review, government agencies in California require a completed initial environmental review, which is most often completed by the applicant but may also be prepared by agency staff or consultants. This initial review is a CEQA-mandated study to determine whether the proposed program or project has the potential to cause adverse impacts. At its most basic level, it is a set of yes or no responses to a checklist of environmental concerns.

If significant effects are found—which the state defines as a "significant effect on the environment" and therefore as "a substantial, or potential substantial, adverse change in any of the physical conditions within the area affected by the project..." (State of California, Public Resources Code Section 21083)—then draft and final environmental impact reports (EIRs) must be prepared. These reports must describe the impacts and also recommend mitigation measures for the significant adverse impact.

When the San Francisco Bay Regional Water Quality Control Board proposed amendments to the region's water-quality control plan, it published its CEQA checklist results on the web for public review and comment (SWRCB 2004). The link included here will take you material that will help better explain the CEQA checklist format (*www.swrcb.ca.gov/rwqcb2/Basin%20Plan/appendix_b_ceqachecklist.doc*).

Figure 2-1. Illustration of a Triggering Event Over Urban Data Layers

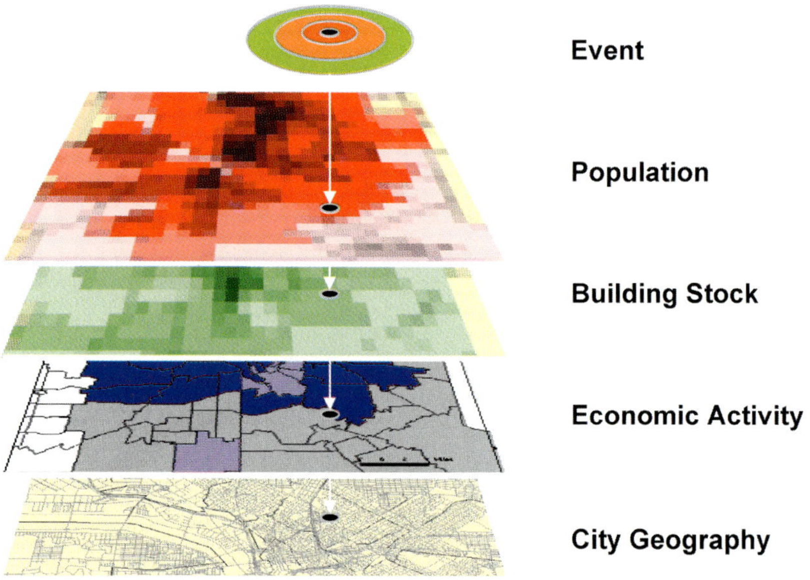

- Event
- Population
- Building Stock
- Economic Activity
- City Geography

Source: Image Courtesy of Risk Management Solutions, Inc.

Risk maps for specific natural and man-made hazards are available in GIS format from a variety of government, academic, and private sources. Similarly, major infrastructure for communities throughout the country is digitally mapped (see discussion of HAZUS below).

GIS USE BY PORTLAND METRO

Metro is the regional government that serves the three counties and 24 cities within the Portland metropolitan region. Under Oregon's state land-use regulations, Metro has key regional land-use responsibilities. It manages the region's urban growth boundary and also developed the region's 2040 growth concept (Metro 2004). In doing so, Metro provides land-use planning services as well as maps and data to businesses, local government, and the region's 1.3 million residents.

The Metro Planning Department's Data Resource Center (DRC) provides state-of-the-art mapping, spatial analysis, regional economic analysis, and demographic forecasting for Metro, its regional partners, businesses, and the public. The DRC is the caretaker of Metro's regional spatial data infrastructure and helps coordinate and link various jurisdictions' data in the region. The Regional Land Information System (RLIS) is a shared version of their GIS system and one of the premier GIS applications to model an urban environment. It was initially developed to support transportation modeling and regional planning applications but has evolved to include input from various local sources. It contains land parcel and tax assessor data, as well as data layers on zoning and planning information, political boundaries, geographic features such as wetlands and soil types, hazard information such as floodplains and landslide-prone areas, and social features such as school districts, bike lanes, and sewage districts. The MetroMap application (www.topaz.metro-region.org/metromap/) is available to the public and allows users to view map-based information about any location in the region. The results can be displayed in either text or map format.

Figure 2-2. A Map from Metro's Data Resource Center

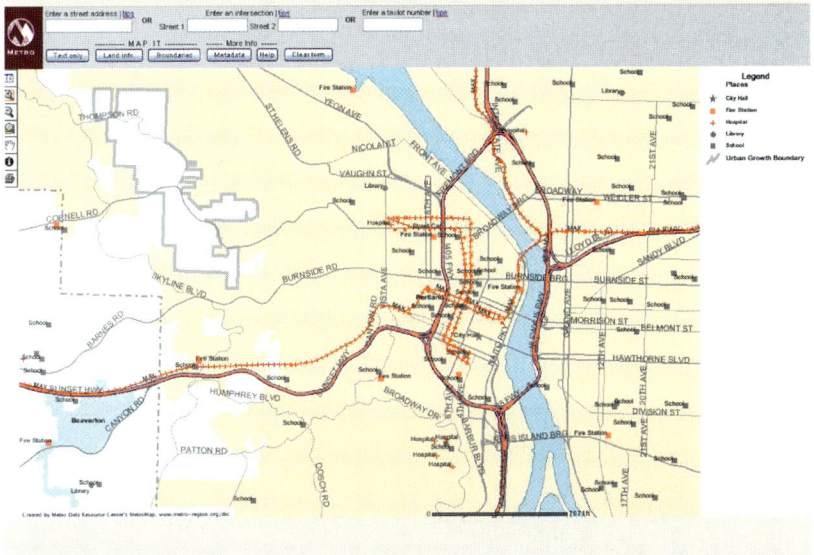

Results of risk identification. At the end the risk identification step, planners should have a list of the potential issues of concern that need further study. This list can then be carried to the next step, *Assessing and Quantifying Risks*, for further analysis.

> **EXPRESSING GOALS AS RISKS IN PIMA COUNTY, ARIZONA**
>
> The Sonoran Desert Conservation Plan (winner of APA's 2002 National Planning Award) grew out of a desire by county supervisors to use science-based evaluation of conservation needs to guide planning efforts rather than political rhetoric. The key values of this plan are stated as follows:
> - Pima County is committed to the long-term survival of the full spectrum of indigenous plants and animals and the conservation of its cultural resources.
> - Riparian resources and aquatic systems are the most vulnerable and least-protected habitats in Pima County.
> - Pima County's mountain parks and natural preserves play an important and diverse role in the life of the community.
> - Pima County is committed to cultural resource conservation so future generations may know the wonders of their past.
> - The conservation of working ranch lands protects vast areas of open space and preserves the heritage and culture of the Southwest.
>
> These values clearly reflect major risks the county faces from growth: species and habitat loss (particularly riparian) and cultural and historical loss (including historical and way-of-life). While these concepts are not expressed as risks in the plan, this example shows how existing planning activities naturally fit with risk management principles and how a "science-driven approach" was used to assess their risks.
>
> Source: www.co.pima.az.us/cmo/sdcp/intro.html

The ability to fully comprehend the trade-offs between risk and reward is the foundation of risk management.

A similar process typically occurs already in most strategic-level planning activities. Key concerns naturally emerge from any broad planning process: issues of concern are currently identified in comprehensive plans, often in the form of goals or values. Applying a risk management framework to planning activities ensures that the complete range of risks potentially affecting a community's welfare is consistently identified and addressed.

Step 2. Assessing and Quantifying Risks

The ability to fully comprehend the trade-offs between risk and reward is the foundation of risk management. Before determining whether and how risks need to be managed, it is necessary to estimate the severity of risks. Some risks can be quantified by probable dollars lost, people killed, jobs displaced per year, or other factors. Other risks cannot be expressed quantifiably and need to be assessed qualitatively in terms such as high, moderate, or low probability of occurrence. Structured approaches are available to assess risk both ways.

A great deal of present-day risk management is focused on the development of tools and the use of probability-based theories for quantifying risks. The natural hazards field has spawned some of the most advanced methods for risk quantification (FEMA 2001; Schwab et al. 1998). Generally speaking, the approach is to calculate the probability of a hazard occurrence by estimating both the frequency and severity of a series of possible natural hazard events. Next, the value of the exposure to these events—typically measured in structures and lives—is assessed, and potential vulnerability, or damageability, of this exposure is then estimated. These calculations can provide an estimate of potential loss for a particular hazard. The insurance industry has made some of the most sophisticated advances in this area, using mathematical applications and software to determine the frequency and severity of various risks to a particular property before insuring it (Risk Management Solutions Inc. 2004; Applied Insurance Research 2004; EQECAT 2004).

Risk assessments can be quantified in different forms. Probabilistic analyses and scenarios are two of the most common.

Probabilistic analyses. Probabilistic analyses determine the likelihood of specific occurrences during a particular time frame. Results can be expressed in many forms. Annualized loss (i.e., the average annual economic or life loss a specific hazard is expected to cause) is a useful presentation. Annualized loss does not predict what losses will occur in any particular year. Instead, it averages out the expected losses for years with severe hazard events with those expected in years with mild or no hazard occurrences.

Scenario analyses. Scenario analyses quantify the effects of a particular event occurring. For example, a "what if" scenario might calculate dollar losses, casualties, and injuries that would occur if a certain hazardous gas was released and formed a plume of a specified size in a specified direction. This is often referred to as a deterministic evaluation of risk.

Scenarios are often a good choice to explain risk to a nontechnical audience, whereas probabilistic analyses produce results that can more easily be compared to losses from other types of risks.

But no land-use decision can escape the fact, as Roger Peilke describes it, that "what is measured is not all that matters, and what matters is not always measured" (Heinz Center 2000). A fully comprehensive risk assessment should attempt to value the physical and environmental impacts of an event, along with quality-of-life, regional, and time-dependent effects. Correlations and accumulations of risks should be identified. Even if only qualitative, the exercise of evaluating the severity and frequency of each potential hazard and the vulnerabilities of exposures can help to provide a common valuation for comparing potential losses.

Characterizing vulnerability. Vulnerability refers to the likelihood of something or someone being harmed or damaged by a specific event or by the cascading impacts of an event on a widespread system or systems. Vulnerability varies with the severity of the risk trigger and is often quantified as a function. It can be expressed in various forms, such as physical damage parameters, dollars of damage caused (i.e., cost of damage relative to replacement cost of building), or lives lost.

The vulnerability of structures and people in the real world has an element of randomness: for example, two houses that are constructed in the same way may be damaged to very different degrees when they experience the same wind pressure. Vulnerability is generally most accurately represented as a range of possible impacts with varying probability. A vulnerability curve actually represents the mean, or most likely, impact state (i.e., percent of building damage) at different levels of hazard (e.g., increasing wind speeds).

Vulnerability can be quantified for physical, economic, and human losses for many types of natural and man-made disasters and particular environmental concerns. For many of the concerns facing communities, less precise determinations of vulnerability must be made.

Tools to assess and quantify risk. Communities have successfully employed the Federal Emergency Management Agency (FEMA) HAZUS computer tool, development impact analyses, and risk matrices to assess and quantify specific and general risks.

> *But no land-use decision can escape the fact, as Roger Peilke describes it, that "what is measured is not all that matters, and what matters is not always measured."*

Many communities are using HAZUS-MH to conduct multihazard risk assessments in compliance with the requirements of the Disaster Mitigation Act of 2000.

- *HAZUS-MH.* One readily available program to quantify natural hazards risk is Hazards-US-Multihazard (HAZUS-MH), a computer tool developed by FEMA and distributed for free that analyzes risk from earthquakes, floods, and hurricane winds (NIBS 2004). HAZUS-MH provides basic inventories of buildings, critical facilities, and infrastructure, including economic value, occupants, and use, in GIS format for all communities in the United States. These databases, developed from national sources, can be updated locally to improve the accuracy of risk estimates. HAZUS-MH can estimate physical damage to buildings and infrastructure, economic losses including repair and reconstruction costs, and social impacts such as deaths and requirements for medical aid. It uses a GIS platform to conduct its analyses. Many communities are using HAZUS-MH to conduct multihazard risk assessments in compliance with the requirements of the Disaster Mitigation Act of 2000 (Srinivasan 2003).

  There are numerous other hazard-specific computer tools to assess risk, such as computer programs that estimate flood damage or the spread of hazardous materials. These tools are available through a variety of government, academic, and private sources in varying price ranges and intended for different users (e.g., government, insurance industry, and researchers).

- *Development impact analyses.* There are many forms of development impact analyses that can be conducted to determine the potential positive and negative outcomes of proposed change or development to a community. These include fiscal impact analyses, socioeconomic impact analyses, and environmental impact analyses, to name a few. Specific procedures have been developed to provide consistent analyses of these concepts, and many consultants offer services or software to assist in this process. Most commonly, communities use fiscal impact analyses in deciding upon proposals for development projects that require rezoning or special use permits.

Projects with negative net fiscal impacts are more likely to be approved than projects with positive fiscal impacts. These negative net fiscal

Figure 2-3. A HAZUS Map Showing Ground-shaking Patterns in Berkeley, California

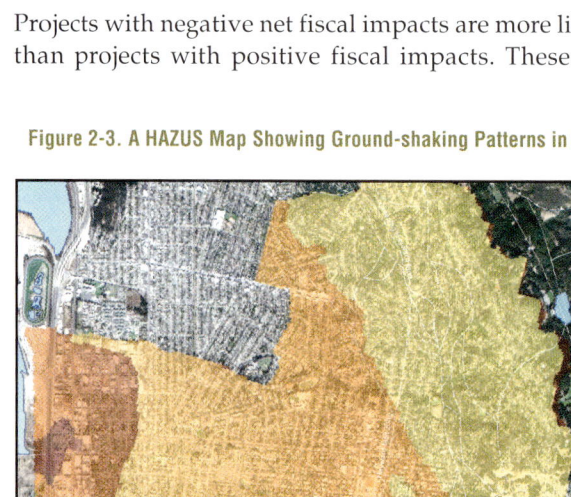

impacts typically consider costs for providing infrastructure and public services versus revenues expected through taxes, fees, and other revenue sources. Where these analyses often fall short is in considering the more indirect and intangible costs and revenues, such as the natural hazard risk and costs, and the impact on regional transportation, economic output, demands for affordable housing, community perceptions, and quality of life. If appropriately expanded, these analyses can be used to compare the impact of different land-use approaches on overall levels of risk.

- *Risk matrices.* A matrix showing risk triggers and their potential impacts on the community can be a guide through the risk assessment process. Table 2-2 is an example chart to help recognize the broad range of both hazards and risks that could relate to land-use decisions. A broad matrix to identify specific risk issues for each community can be a guide during a comprehensive planning process. It can also be used to comprehensively assess and display decisions about acceptable risk thresholds. For a particular development proposal, the matrix can be slimmed down to include only relevant triggers and risks. After identifying which risks on the matrix should be assessed, the output of an analysis can be presented in the matrix to guide decision making. Judgments of low, medium, and high risk can be expressed visually in this format.

Results of risk assessment. Risk is determined by combining the numerical or qualitative characterizations of hazard, exposure, and vulnerability. The output of this process will be expressed as the probable loss of dollars, lives, acres of wetland, or other measurable categories, or it can be expressed using a qualitative description such as *severe impact*.

A comprehensive risk assessment may include the evaluation of different types of risks and risks from different sources, and the output may be in a variety of formats with differing levels of certainty. Putting all of the pieces together to identify the greatest risks can be a challenge. Constructing a matrix to present your findings on all risks in one graphical format can help. This requires risks expressed in a diverse range of formats, including numerical output of different units and nonnumerical categorizations, to be translated into a common format, such as *low, medium,* and *high* risk. This translation necessarily incorporates community-specific judgments and values

The output also needs to be formatted so that it can be readily understood by and communicated to the audience or stakeholders, thereby increasing its utility in the decision-making process. All too frequently poorly presented output can alienate non-scientific decision makers—whether they are policymakers, planners, or community members—and reduces its effectiveness in risk management. Consider the following five steps to better ensure that an audience or stakeholder will receive and use the results of a risk assessment:

- Hear—the audience needs to physically access the output

- Understand—the audience needs to understand the technical language of the assessment

- Believe—both the communicator and the output need to be credible

- Personalize—those receiving the assessment data need to understand how it affects them personally

- Act—once these steps are taken, the audience, or recipient of the results, can more rapidly move through a decision-making process

Risk is determined by combining the numerical or qualitative characterizations of hazard, exposure, and vulnerability.

Table 2-2.
Sample Risk Matrix

Triggering Events

Risks to Community Elements	Earthquake	Flood	Landslide	Wildfire	Hurricane	Tsunami	Drought	Coastal Erosion	Tornado	Terrorism event	Large power outage	Chemical spill	Hazardous gas release	Effluent spill	Industrial explosion	Cyber terrorism/virus	Jobs/Housing imbalance	Industry downturn	Urban sprawl	Crime
Capital Risks																				
Damage to government buildings																				
Damage to essential facilities																				
Damage to residences																				
Damage to lifelines/utilities																				
Damage to transportation systems																				
Damage to machinery/equipment																				
Damage to furnishings																				
Loss of inventory																				
Damage to crops																				
Loss of function of facilities																				
Environmental Risks																				
Water pollution																				
Air pollution																				
Loss of biodiversity																				
Disruption of wildlife																				
Noise pollution																				
Light pollution																				
Loss of natural beauty																				
Social/Cultural Risks																				
Loss of life																				
Injury/Illness																				
Loss of residence																				
Loss of cultural/historical resources																				
Demographic change																				
Impacts on vulnerable populations																				
Change in neighborhood character																				
Economic Risks																				
Financial loss to government																				
Financial loss to business																				
Financial loss to residents																				
Reduced tax income																				
Reduced business income																				
Increased government expenditures																				
Lack of affordable housing																				
Loss of high paying jobs																				
Institutional and Policy Risks																				
Liability																				
Damage to reputation																				
Staff turnover																				
Erosion of vision and goals																				
Increased distrust of government																				
Undermining of other policies																				

Step 3. Making and implementing risk management decisions

The real benefit of risk identification and quantification is to inform decision making. As is demonstrated daily by the financial and insurance industries, the quantitative analyses of risk management allow people to make more informed decisions and, frequently, to take more risk than they otherwise would. These industries look at a suite of decision options analyzed with risk management techniques and frequently create a package solution that diversifies and distributes the risk. In other words, they design a portfolio of risks unlikely to have adverse impacts on the company from any one event or over any short period of time.

Risk management approaches. There are four basic options for managing risks: avoidance or elimination, reduction or mitigation, sharing, and retention (Reiss 2001). The challenge in risk decision making is not finding *the* solution but finding *the best* solution. The best solution depends on the circumstances, values, and priorities of the decision makers. Table 2-3 provides examples of land-use-related risk management decision options.

- *Risk avoidance or elimination.* This option involves the complete avoidance or elimination of a risk. Avoiding or eliminating a risk can entail removing a risk trigger or deciding not to pursue a project that introduces new risks. Although avoidance is highly effective, it is often impractical or undesirable, either because the public agency is legally required to engage in some aspect of the risk or because there is some overriding consideration beneficial to the community. Some risks, such as damage from earthquakes, are not technically possible to eliminate at this time: we cannot stop earthquakes from occurring and cannot design structures guaranteed to survive their shaking undamaged. Elimination is closely linked with risk identification. Once a risk is known and if the potential costs exceed an acceptable level, elimination, if possible and affordable, may be the best course of action.

- *Risk reduction or mitigation.* These strategies usually reduce the frequency or severity of the potential losses resulting from a risk by changing physical characteristics or operations, or both. Mitigation is a term familiar to those involved in environmental and natural hazard management. Example mitigation decisions include buyouts to move homes from floodplains or "no net loss" projects for wetland habitat protection.

- *Risk sharing or transfer.* These strategies shift the risk-bearing responsibility to another party, and that party then takes on the responsibility for handling any losses. Insurance is a classic example of an economic risk transfer technique. During the land development process, the streets, sidewalks, and other infrastructure built as part of the project are deeded to local agencies. As part of this transfer, local agencies then assume the maintenance costs and associated risks for infrastructure and services.

- *Risk retention.* Public agencies retain risk when they choose to fund potential losses, either wholly or partially, with their own resources. The most visible form of risk retention is self-insurance that communities knowingly accept. For example, electing not to insure city-owned buildings for potential damage from floods means those risks are self-insured. More commonly, risk is retained unknowingly because governments, businesses, and residents are unaware of it. Even after a risk management strategy is undertaken, there still may be some residual risk. This residual risk can also be assessed and further managed, such as transferring it through insurance.

There are four basic options for managing risks: avoidance or elimination, reduction or mitigation, sharing, and retention.

Table 2-3.
Examples of Specific Risk Management Approaches

	Avoid or Eliminate	Reduce or Mitigate	Share or Transfer	Retain
Capital Stock Risks	– Prohibit development – Buyout or relocate structure to no hazard zone – Destroy structure	– Strengthen structure's ability to resist hazard – Change use or occupancy pattern of structure – Enforce stricter zoning and building standards – Develop response plans and improve hazard warning systems – Build redundant infrastructure systems – Secure items against damage or theft	– Develop alternate locations for key functions – Institute a geologic hazard abatement district where homeowners share in future landslide repair costs – Real estate hazard disclosures	– Take no action – Self-insure the stock – Treat physical losses as expenses
Environmental Risks	– Eliminate point sources of pollution – Mandate use of specific technologies (e.g., emissions-free vehicles) – Enforce strict zoning standards	– Eliminate point sources of pollution – Launch clean-up efforts – Regulate use and storage of potential pollutants – Reduce development densities in most sensitive areas – Habitat conservation plans – Incentives for use of specific technologies – Incentives for desirable development decisions	– Develop transfer or development rights programs, or environmental land swaps	– Take no action – Brownfield cleanup and reuse costs
Economic Risks	– Avoid or eliminate capital stock risk – Mandate "smart growth" – Develop business retention and job placement programs	– Incentives to mitigate or reduce risk – Diversify income sources – Attract a wide range of business types – Avoid or mitigate environmental risks to income-generating sites (e.g., tourist attractions) – Incentives for smart growth – Build economic alliances/partnerships	– Shared responsibilities between government and business community (i.e., BIDs)	– Take no action – Pre-arrange special funds or line of credit for lost revenues
Social and Cultural Risks	– Deny occupancy of hazardous buildings – Protect cultural assets through zoning standards	– Integrate sociocultural indicators into risk assessment – Fund hospitals and social services mitigation and planning – Identify and serve pre- and post-disaster needs of vulnerable populations (e.g., elderly, handicapped, immigrants)	– Provide incentives for homeowners, renters, and businesses to purchase insurance – Create mutual aid agreements	– Take no action – Prepare shelter plans for displaced residents
Institutional and Policy Risks	– Close public access to potential terrorist targets – Citizen involvement in risk management planning	– Engage in collaborative planning and decision making – Launch education campaigns – Link community goals to development decision making	– Purchase liability insurance – Join insurance pool	– Take no action – Self-insure against liability

Table 2-4.
Sample of Stakeholder Groups for Risk Decision Making

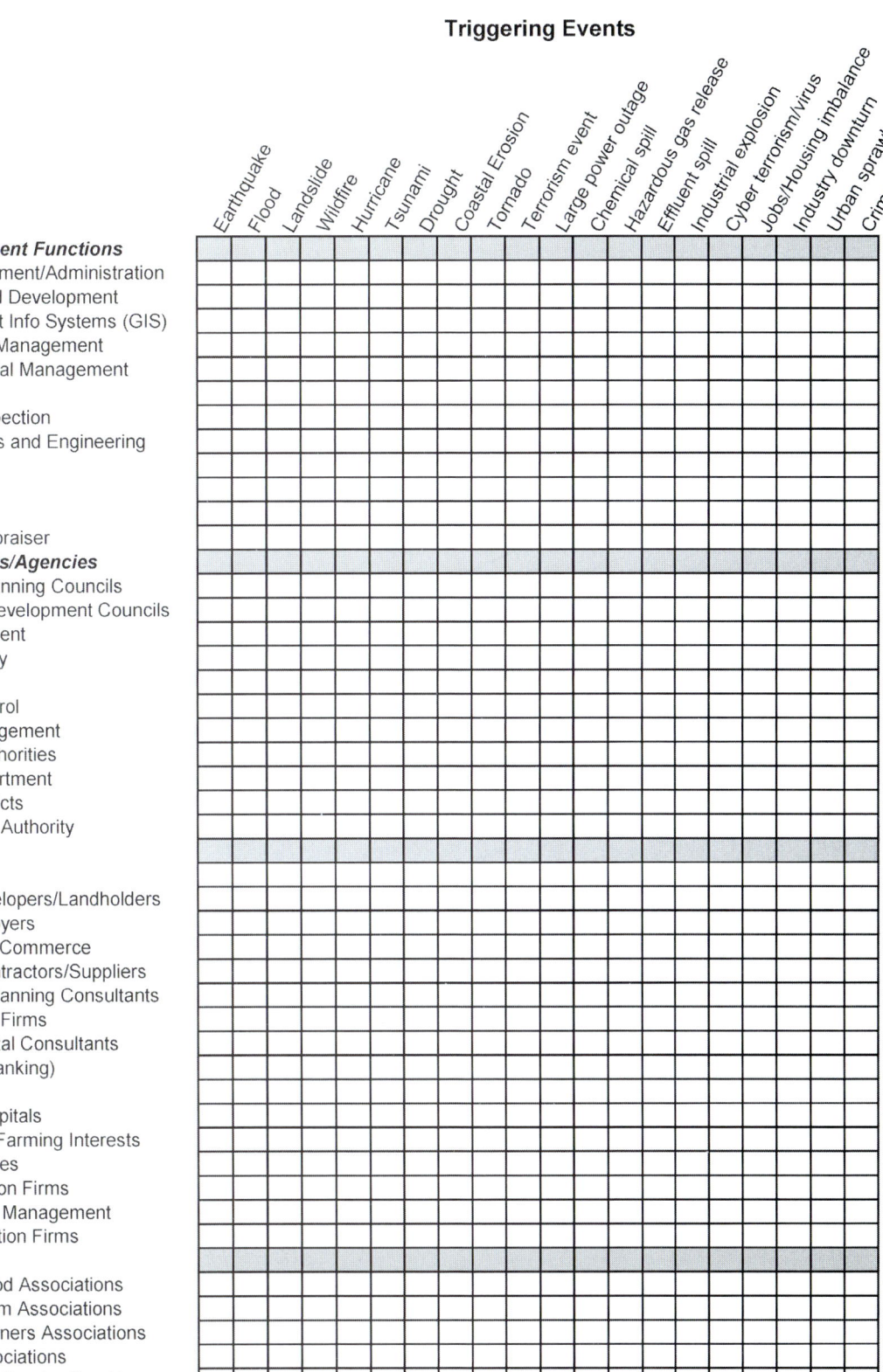

Determining acceptable risk thresholds. In deciding upon risk management approaches, each community (or other decision-making body) must first consciously decide what levels of risk are acceptable for them to bear and what levels need to be addressed. Broad principles, such as community goals in comprehensive plans, are an essential part of defining risk acceptability thresholds. Many decisions, however, need to be made project by project, as the costs of bearing and managing risk are determined. Acceptable risk thresholds will vary by community and may change with time. Table 2-4 lists the variety of stakeholder groups and organizations that should be involved in defining risk thresholds.

Tools for risk management decisions. The range of activities, tools, and techniques to manage risks is as broad as the array of risks and the diversity among those communities. The best risk management strategies are often creative, unique policies and programs designed by and for a local group. Examining steps similar communities have taken can be the best way to start defining what would and would not work for your own risks. The case studies presented in Chapter 3 offer a small sample of risk management strategies for a variety of issues from a diverse set of communities.

- *Plot a risk map.* Risk mapping is another method for quantifying the impact of individual risks and for making communitywide risk decisions. As illustrated in Figure 2-4, a risk plot, or map, can then be used to segregate potential losses into categories according to frequency and severity (Reiss 2001). A simple risk map may include only four categories:
    1. High frequency/high severity
    2. High frequency/low severity
    3. Low frequency/low severity
    4. Low frequency/high severity.

A more complex approach could add a third dimension, such as predictability or understanding. A community might decide, for example, that the low-frequency/low-severity risks are well understood, and therefore these risks will be retained. Low-frequency/high-severity events, on the other hand, are often less predictable and very good candidates for risk transfer mechanisms, like insurance or bonds.

The range of activities, tools, and techniques to manage risks is as broad as the array of risks and the diversity among those communities.

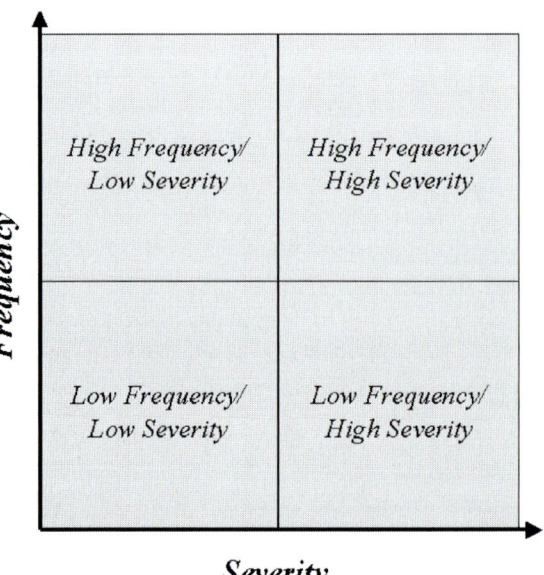

Figure 2-4. Sample Risk Map

- *Cost-benefit analyses.* A common tool used to assist risk decision making is a cost-benefit analysis. This type of analysis is most useful when acceptable risk thresholds have already been defined, such as a specific cost-benefit ratio that necessitates action. Many government agencies, such as FEMA, require a cost-benefit analysis that must use their procedures and be submitted with grant applications when those grants are related to risk management activities. A cost-benefit analysis assesses whether the costs of a proposed risk management scheme are higher or lower than the probable future costs that will occur due to the risk if no action or a different action is taken. All costs are typically expressed in financial terms, and it can be difficult to include nonquantifiable impacts, such as quality of life, in these calculations. The costs and benefits of alternate management strategies can be evaluated and compared as part of the decision-making process.

- *Planning procedures and regulations.* Many of the tools used to implement risk management decisions are the same tools that planners use on a routine basis. At a strategic level, comprehensive or general planning efforts can provide broad policy goals and directions for risk management activities. These goals and policy decisions have acceptable risk thresholds embedded in them. Subdivision regulations, building codes, development standards, and occupancy and zoning regulations are tools at a tactical, project-specific level to implement the risk management visions expressed in these policy goals. Applying these techniques with a risk management framework allows for systematic, consistent decision making on risks and opens a wide range of decision options to communities.

Results of the risk management decision-making process. Ultimately, a key result of a risk decision-making process is confidence the risks the community chooses to hold are acceptable given their values. This will come from a set of policies and implementation procedures defining the approaches to be used to manage specific types of risk. When used in land development decisions, a risk-based framework will challenge communities to consider the full range of potential consequences as well as the alternatives for avoiding, reducing, or controlling them. With a well-managed risk management process, little risk will be unintentionally retained and the community will explicitly understand what risks it retains.

Step 4. Monitoring and Implementation over Time

Local public agencies are relative newcomers to monitoring and evaluation, and this important feedback loop is often overlooked or underfunded (Seasons 2003). Monitoring and long-term implementation are continuous, ongoing, critical aspects of the risk management process. They provide a means for checking and ensuring that risk management strategies are working. Monitoring and implementation programs should review the following:

- Are risk reduction strategies being implemented as envisioned? If not, what can be done to mandate or provide sufficient incentives for implementation?

- Is the selected risk management strategy working? Is risk being reduced to a level acceptable to the community? If not, what additional risk management strategies are needed?

- Is the risk reduction strategy working over time? How can the effectiveness of risk reduction strategies be evaluated at regular intervals? In the long term, do risk management approaches remain relevant and effective?

- Are changes in the community, such as demographic or economic shifts, being reflected in risk reduction strategies and local plan updates?

MONITORING ENVIRONMENTAL MITIGATION IN CALIFORNIA

CEQA, as profiled, has required review and mitigation of all significant environmental impacts of development in California since the 1970s. A substantial public review process is also mandated in the act, and all relevant state and other regulatory agencies must be integrated into the review process by the lead agency. Once all comments are received and revisions made, the lead agency must then decide whether to (a) conclude the impacts cannot be mitigated and the project is denied, or (b) approve the project with mitigation measures and a statement of "overriding considerations." This statement declares that the benefits of the project outweigh and therefore "override" its potential adverse impacts. This statement, in other words, defines the amount of risk the lead agency considers acceptable.

By the close of its first decade of existence, state legislators and agency officials recognized that the legislation did not ensure that the mitigation measures adopted by lead agencies were actually implemented during the course of the project. In 1988, the California Senate passed a bill requiring a lead agency to "adopt a reporting and monitoring program for the changes to the project," which it adopted or conditionally approved in order to mitigate or avoid significant environmental effects (AEP 2000, 3). In addition to requiring monitoring, the legislation was also intended to provide a "feedback loop" so that mitigation measures might be modified if they were determined to be infeasible during monitoring (AEP 2000, 8).

Unfortunately, the requirements for reporting and monitoring were vague, and a 1992 survey of 166 public agencies in the state suggested the manner in which local agencies complied with the requirements varied considerably (AEP 2000, 6). In 1998, when the state's CEQA Guidelines were finally amended to include monitoring and reporting requirements, they provided a clearer distinction between reporting and monitoring and when and how monitoring plans should be developed. A follow-up survey in 1999 of 169 planning department directors in the state found the attitudes toward mitigation monitoring and reporting had improved and monitoring had been institutionalized within most planning departments (AEP 2000, 8). Furthermore, the feedback loop was also being established: one-third of the agencies surveyed had some procedure in place for modifying mitigation measures that were not working (AEP 2000, 8)

Tools for monitoring and implementation. Tools for monitoring include worksheets and implementation requirements to periodically review specific programs.

- *Monitoring worksheets.* A program for monitoring the implementation of risk management measures should contain at least the following components:

    1. A list of specific risk management measures adopted by the agency

    2. A schedule for regularly checking on compliance with the measures, including progress toward meeting specified standards, if any

    3. A means of recording compliance at the time of each check

    4. A statement assigning responsibility for monitoring implementation of the measures to specific persons or agencies, public or private

5. If monitoring duties are contracted to private individuals or firms, provisions for ensuring that monitoring reflects the independent judgment of the public agency

6. Provisions for funding monitoring activities, including the imposition of fees

7. Provisions for responding to a failure to comply with any required measure.

A worksheet can be a convenient way to comply with monitoring regulations. Worksheets can be used to express the:

1. impact being mitigated;

2. mitigation measure for that impact;

3. implementer;

4. monitor;

5. monitoring requirements;

6. frequency of monitoring or reporting;

7. standards for completion or compliance; and

8. verification of compliance

While the program is a relatively simple one, a checklist rather than a worksheet may suffice to guide inspections, record findings, and certify compliance.

- *Implementation requirements.* Environmental mitigation monitoring and reporting guidelines often explicitly: define the relative roles of involved agencies, staff, and project proponents; establish administrative procedures; provide a standardized format for reporting or monitoring programs; establish general timetables; outline public comment and review procedures; and provide or identify enforcement mechanisms (State of California 1996).

Standardizing the framework for monitoring and reporting promotes consistency and thoroughness in development activities.

Monitoring compliance can be required as a condition of project approval or, if a framework ordinance is in place, by reference to that ordinance. Enforcement authority can be conferred through other planning mechanisms, including local zoning, subdivision, and related land-use regulations. Typically, enforcement procedures are enacted by ordinance and provide for administrative dispute resolution. Project monitors, whether agency staff, private developers, or contract personnel, should be given clear written guidance for monitoring and reporting.

Results of monitoring and evaluation. Standardizing the framework for monitoring and reporting promotes consistency and thoroughness in development activities. In order to maximize efficiency in implementing a monitoring or reporting program, every effort should be made to integrate the requirements of the program into current land-use regulations and inspection procedures. This applies whether the program is comprehensive or project specific. As a general rule, the more that risk management programs can use existing procedures and requirements, the easier those programs will be to implement. The more that such programs work outside usual procedures, the more expensive and difficult they may be to implement.

SUMMARY

The basic framework to manage risks—identification, assessment, decision making, and monitoring—is flexible enough to respond to the variety of issues that threaten the well-being of diverse communities. Structured approaches exist within various disciplines to assist the process. New interdisciplinary approaches are also being encouraged, explored, and documented. This framework can be applied in many different ways, depending on community needs and resources. However it is used, your community will reap the most benefits by applying an appropriate risk management process *consistently* for all major land-use decisions over time.

The next chapter takes an in-depth look at four different programs around the country that incorporate risk management principles. As the next chapter shows, while the basic steps of risk management remain the same, the implementation approach that works will differ for every community.

CHAPTER 3

Examining Four Programs to Manage Risks

Planners are often painted in the colors of frustration—as having marvelous plans but facing insuperable obstacles. The search for more effective tools to implement the plans, therefore, continues.

The International City Managers Association (ICMA)

There is no better way to learn about risk management than to examine the implementation of real programs. This chapter presents programs from around the country in which risk management has been incorporated into land-use decision making. These examples give insights into what approaches have and have not worked in practice, issues that have been stumbling blocks for various jurisdictions, and different ways that risk management tools and techniques can be applied. They illustrate how risks can be managed through land-use policies and plans at both the strategic and practical implementation levels. These four case studies address different types of risks in different ways, and each has its particular successes and failures.

- Case Study 1: Berkeley, California, shows how a jurisdiction can leverage federal and state mandates to build political support for natural hazard risk management.

- Case Study 2: Palm Beach County, Florida, shows how the county responded to state mandates to incorporate growth management in its ongoing planning by trying a variety of institutional approaches before finding one that allowed cities and the county to collaborate effectively.

- Case Study 3: Calvert County, Maryland, demonstrates how an incentive-based program to encourage communities to reduce sprawl and its associated impact can play a role in reducing risks.

- Case Study 4: Saint Paul, Minnesota, considers the regional tax-sharing program in Minnesota aimed to reduce risks stemming from increased fiscal and developmental disparities between cities in the Twin Cities metro region and examines how it has affected local land-use decisions.

Figure 3-1. The Berkeley, California, Region

The city's risk management goals were codified into city policy and incorporated into the way the city's planning department makes land-use decisions.

DISASTER-RESISTANT BERKELEY: UNITING DISASTER MANAGEMENT WITH PLANNING IN CALIFORNIA

Berkeley, California, has been concerned about the risks from natural disasters for many years but until recently approached this risk on a project-by-project basis. As funding became available to tackle one aspect of the city's risk, a discrete project would be launched to address that issue. In recent years, the city has been working hard to unite its disaster management efforts into a coordinated approach that can be consistently applied over time. City staff found that linking the requirements of two mandates, one state and one federal, united its disaster management efforts with its comprehensive planning. The city's risk management goals were codified into city policy and incorporated into the way the city's planning department makes land-use decisions.

The city has been concerned about natural disaster with good reason. It straddles the Hayward Fault, which experts suggest has a 27 percent probability of experiencing a major earthquake by 2033 (USGS 2003). The city, built-up primarily before World War II, consists of buildings and infrastructure mostly constructed without the benefit of modern engineering and construction know-how, and therefore vulnerable to significant damage in the next major quake. In addition to earthquakes, the city borders an undeveloped wildland area that is at extreme risk to wildfires. This was tragically demonstrated in 1991 when a major conflagration burned out of control on its borders for more than 48 hours, destroying 62 homes in the city and burning hundreds more in neighboring Oakland. City leaders and residents have grown increasingly aware that the city's values are threatened by these major hazards and its character could irrevocably change unless significant steps are taken to reduce this threat.

In the past few decades, the city has engaged in a patchwork of disaster mitigation and preparedness programs. These programs include strengthening particular city buildings, such as fire stations and schools, with bond and grant funding. They also encompass innovative incentive schemes, such as a partial refund of the city's property transfer tax if residents use the funds to upgrade the property's disaster safety. These two programs and many others launched by the city played an important role in reducing the city's risk to natural disasters, but they were conducted independently and were at risk of being undermined when city staff changed or a funding source ran dry. Most of these risk management efforts were being pushed through by a couple of champions for this cause. These people recognized that the city's disaster management activities needed to be separated from individuals and institutionalized in ongoing city programs.

Uniting Two Mandates
The state of California mandates that all communities prepare general plans (the equivalent elsewhere of comprehensive plans) incorporating numerous topics or "elements," including elements focusing on housing, open-space, conservation, and disaster preparedness. All California communities are required to include seven core planning elements in their general plans: land use, circulation, housing, conservation, open-space, noise, and safety (California Government Code Sections 65300 et seq.). The Berkeley General Plan underwent a massive revision, which was adopted in 2003, and examined each of these subjects in detail through thousands of hours of community meetings and in-depth involvement from the city's many boards and commissions. During this process, city staff became aware of an impending federal requirement to prepare a hazard mitigation plan and worked to coordinate the two planning processes.

In 2000, Congress passed the Disaster Mitigation Act of 2000 (44 CFR 201.6). This act aims to greatly increase incentives at all levels of government to engage in cost-saving mitigation activities before disasters occur. The act requires all jurisdictions that could potentially receive federal disaster funds, including states, counties, cities, and territories, to prepare a comprehensive Local Hazard Mitigation Plan prior to a disaster event. This plan must meet Federal Emergency Management Agency (FEMA) guidelines and be approved by FEMA. Jurisdictions with approved plans will be eligible for pre- and post-disaster grants for mitigation and specific types of response activities; those without cannot receive such funds. This funding change took effect on November 1, 2004.

By coordinating the general and mitigation plan processes, Berkeley was able to make the two plans consistent and complementary. Disaster risk management issues were woven throughout the general plan. For example, the land-use and housing elements identify zoning policies that could cause potential problems for affordable housing after a major disaster. (See the following section for a description of the specific problems.) The policies in the disaster mitigation plan flow directly from those of the general plan, with more details about implementation. The disaster mitigation plan was included as an appendix to the general plan, ensuring that in the future both plans will be revised at the same time, using the same process. This way, the two plans will always be coordinated and consistent. Berkeley has adopted procedures to review and monitor the risk management issues in these plans every two years.

By coordinating the general and mitigation plan processes, Berkeley was able to make the two plans consistent and complementary.

The city's general plan and mitigation plan work to reduce the risk of sudden loss of numerous affordable housing units through many policy avenues.

Implementing Risk Policies Through Land Use

Coordinating disaster management plans with the city's comprehensive plans allowed policies to be developed and implemented that address risks from multiple angles. The multipronged approach the city is now pursuing to reduce the risk of sudden loss of significant amounts of affordable housing due to an earthquake provides a good example of the benefits of a united planning effort. This problem, although focused on housing, requires efforts from many different city departments to be effectively overcome.

The risk assessment undertaken by the city as part of its mitigation planning effort identified that affordable housing units were disproportionately located in structures known to be at risk of collapse in earthquakes, including structural types referred to as *soft story* and *unreinforced masonry* (Berkeley 2004). In addition, because the city had instituted "downzoning" policies in the 1960s after numerous multiunit buildings were built in primarily single-family neighborhoods, angering residents with the way neighborhood character changed without their input, allowable densities in multifamily zones were reduced (Berkeley 2003). By including people with a diverse range of backgrounds in the mitigation planning process, it was clear that the city faced risks far greater than merely losing housing units: the city demographics, diversity, and character could radically change after a major earthquake, particularly considering high real-estate values in these single-family neighborhoods. Major rehabilitations would have to conform to the lower-density zoning standards, so landowners could not build multiunit housing to replace lost housing. Furthermore, private landowners would have overwhelming economic incentives to replace damaged and destroyed older apartment buildings with luxury condominiums or other high-income developments. Recognizing that a core community value in Berkeley is diversity, policy makers and community members agreed this risk needed to be addressed.

The city's general plan and mitigation plan work to reduce the risk of sudden loss of numerous affordable housing units through many policy avenues. The issue is being addressed from a technical perspective by preparing standards for seismically upgrading the types of structures of most concern and trying to reduce barriers of homeowners to the engineering knowledge required to strengthen these types of buildings (Berkeley 2004, policy A-5; Berkeley 2003, policy S-20). The city's Rent Control Board is examining the potential use of economic incentives to upgrade existing affordable housing (Berkeley 2003, policy H-15). Further, multiple policies are being implemented to encourage the construction of new affordable housing that meets current stringent design and construction codes. These include zoning changes to provide density bonuses for affordable housing units, to encourage affordable housing construction above commercial properties, and to promote infill development in single-family residential areas (Berkeley 2003, Policies LU-3, 18, and 25). While the problem of at-risk affordable housing remains formidable, the city hopes this integrated approach will reduce the risk over time.

Berkeley prepared both its general plan and local hazard mitigation plan in response to state and federal mandates. Having these activities mandated forced policy makers to focus on the problems and make them priorities on their busy agendas. Beyond the mandates, however, city staff and leaders recognized that these activities could be used to the city's benefit, particularly if they were coordinated so that they could most effectively tackle issues of importance to the city. Berkeley launched a coordinated planning process specifically meeting its own community priorities that went beyond policy requirements. In this way, the city has institutionalized plans and implementation measures for disaster-related outcomes in its official policies, zoning laws, rent board procedures, building codes, and other tools to address risks, including risks to affordable housing and numerous other disaster-related concerns that were highlighted through this process. Most importantly, the benefits of the city's patchwork of mitigation programs have been preserved in policy and now go beyond finite programs that depend on individuals.

PALM BEACH COUNTY: THE FRONT LINES FOR FLORIDA'S ONGOING GROWTH MANAGEMENT EFFORTS

Slightly larger than 2,020 square miles, Palm Beach County is one of Florida's largest counties and one of its most politically complex. There are more than 39 municipalities in Palm Beach County, ranging from the wealthy, coastal paradise of the City of Palm Beach to the agricultural hamlet of Belle Glade, 45 miles to the west of Palm Beach near Lake Okeechobee. The county is increasingly threatened by sprawl as its population booms. Its population of more than 1 million almost tripled since the 1970s and is expected to reach nearly 1.43 million by 2020.

Florida's mild climate, natural beauty, and bountiful resources drew millions of people in the decades following World War II, moving it from the twentieth to the eighth largest state by 1975. A severe drought and resulting water shortage in the early 1970s forced legislative and gubernatorial leaders to enact statewide comprehensive planning legislation and mandate local governments to be consistent with the state plan goals (DeGrove 1992). Complying with this legislation, Palm Beach County adopted its first comprehensive plan and supporting regulations in 1970 (Palm Beach County 2003).

Unfortunately, this initial effort to coordinate planning at the local and state levels was unsuccessful, and local governments strongly opposed the mandates. Florida's Governor Askew and the legislature persisted, however, and passed another version of the state planning act in 1975. It also required local comprehensive plans but did not provide guidelines, funds, or standards; the state also had no means to enforce local plan consistency with the state guidelines (Burby and May 1997).

The Evolution of Florida's Growth Management System

As unbridled growth continued throughout the state, environmentalists helped launch a second growth management campaign in the early 1980s. In response, Governor Bob Graham formed the second Environmental Land Management Study Committee in 1982 and strategically involved a broad cross section of stakeholders (Burby and May 1997). The committee's 1984 report defined what it believed would be a stronger policy and implementation framework for state planning (DeGrove 1984). The State and

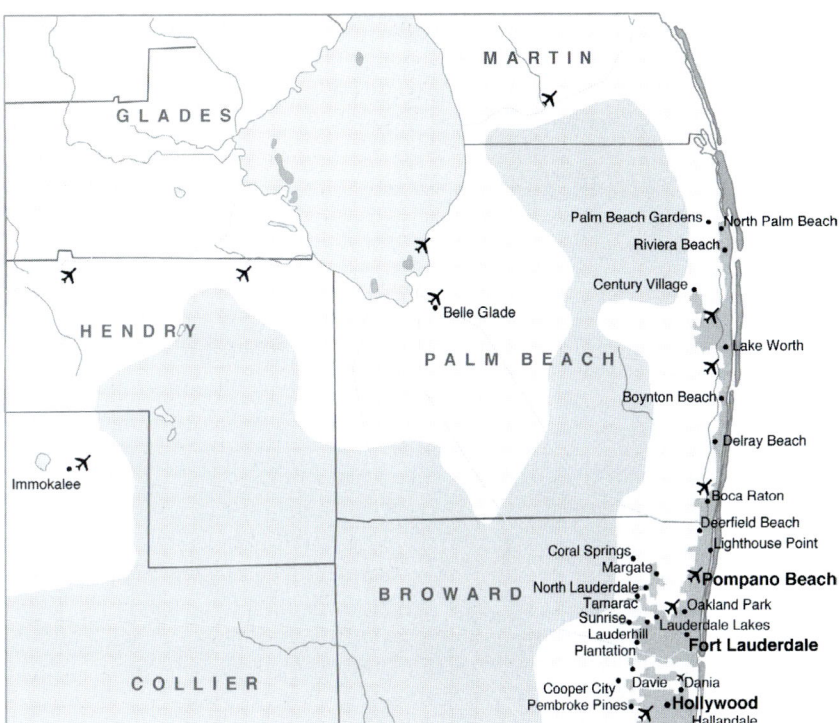

Figure 3-2. The Palm Beach County, Florida, Region

Regional Planning Act of 1984 emerged from this process as Florida's second-generation growth management legislation (DeGrove 1992). It mandated that the governor develop a state comprehensive plan that was adopted by the legislature in 1985. The 1984 legislation also required state agencies to adopt functional plans, and the 11 regional comprehensive plans all had to be developed in consistency with the state plan. Ample funding was granted to regional planning councils, and as a result, by 1987, all 11 region plans had been prepared.

A long sought-after, multilevel planning framework was finally adopted in 1985 requiring all local governments to develop plans consistent with state and regional plans (DeGrove 1992). The 1985 legislation also added a final hook: all plans were required to be periodically revised and updated (every seven years), and local governments that did not comply were sanctioned. The state helped ensure success by tasking the state's Department of Community Affairs (DCA) to provide technical assistance and funds to local governments for planning. DCA also developed model plans and model land development codes to assist local governments in their efforts. By 1992, all 457 cities and counties had adopted comprehensive plans (Burby and May 1997).

The new process remained largely intact until 1991, when Governor Lawton Chiles established a growth management task force to evaluate the state's progress. It found that linkages between state budgeting and planning were not complete, and the state plan had not been updated regularly (Burby and May 1997). A new crop of legislation, addressing the task force's concerns, was adopted on the final day of the state's 1993 legislative session. Among other issues, the legislation required that the state comprehensive plan be reviewed every two years, and requirements for intergovernmental coordination were strengthened.

The Struggle to Succeed

Palm Beach County struggled to respond to the state's 1985 requirement to adopt a local comprehensive plan consistent with state and regional plans. At the time, Palm Beach County was experiencing extraordinary growth, and a number of cities and special service districts were being created. Overlapping annexations and jurisdictional land-use conflicts highlighted the poor communication and coordination among cities and undermined the county's planning efforts (de Aragon 1996).

In 1986, voters amended the county's charter to create the Palm Beach County Council to coordinate the land-use planning process and, ultimately, to deliver a countywide future land-use element. The council was charged with analyzing incompatible aspects of proposed development projects and enforcing plan consistency across the county (de Aragon 1996). As the council evolved and asserted itself more into local planning and development processes, cities grew increasingly worried and resentful about losing their land-use control. Cities in Palm Beach County rebelled against the council's attempted interference in local land-use policy and voters eventually dissolved the council in 1992. But as this council's efforts unraveled, Palm Beach County planning interests did not give up and carefully studied their mistakes. The county was finally able to adopt a revised comprehensive plan in August 1989 that was consistent with state and regional plans as defined in the state's 1985 legislation.

In 1997, the county created a 49-member task force to work cooperatively with cities in a new planning process. Over the next two years, the task force led more than 22 focus-group meetings, 28 half-day meetings with a policy development task force, 12 public workshops, and three public hearings (Meck 2000). It also complied with the state's stringent land-use and growth management mandates requiring plan consistency and review, and it gained the backing of both pro-development and environmental advocates.

The results of the county's efforts were literally rewarding. In April 2000, Palm Beach County won the American Planning Association (APA) Current Topic Award for Growing Smart Initiatives and Applications (Meck 2000). The award focused on Palm Beach County's future land-use plan, The Managed Growth Tier System (MGTS), which was adopted by the county's Board of Commissioners in August 1999 as an amendment to the county's comprehensive plan. The MGTS defines five distinct land-use regions, or tiers: urban-suburban, exurban, rural, agricultural reserve, and the Glades. The county's planning policy framework steers the bulk (90 percent) of the county's projected growth to the urban-suburban tier, and the county's Future Land Use Element also defines density bonuses and other zoning incentives to encourage development to locate in this tier (Palm Beach County 2003).

In April 2000, Palm Beach County won the American Planning Association (APA) Current Topic Award for Growing Smart Initiatives and Applications.

Figure 3-3. A Map Showing Palm Beach County's Managed Growth Tier System

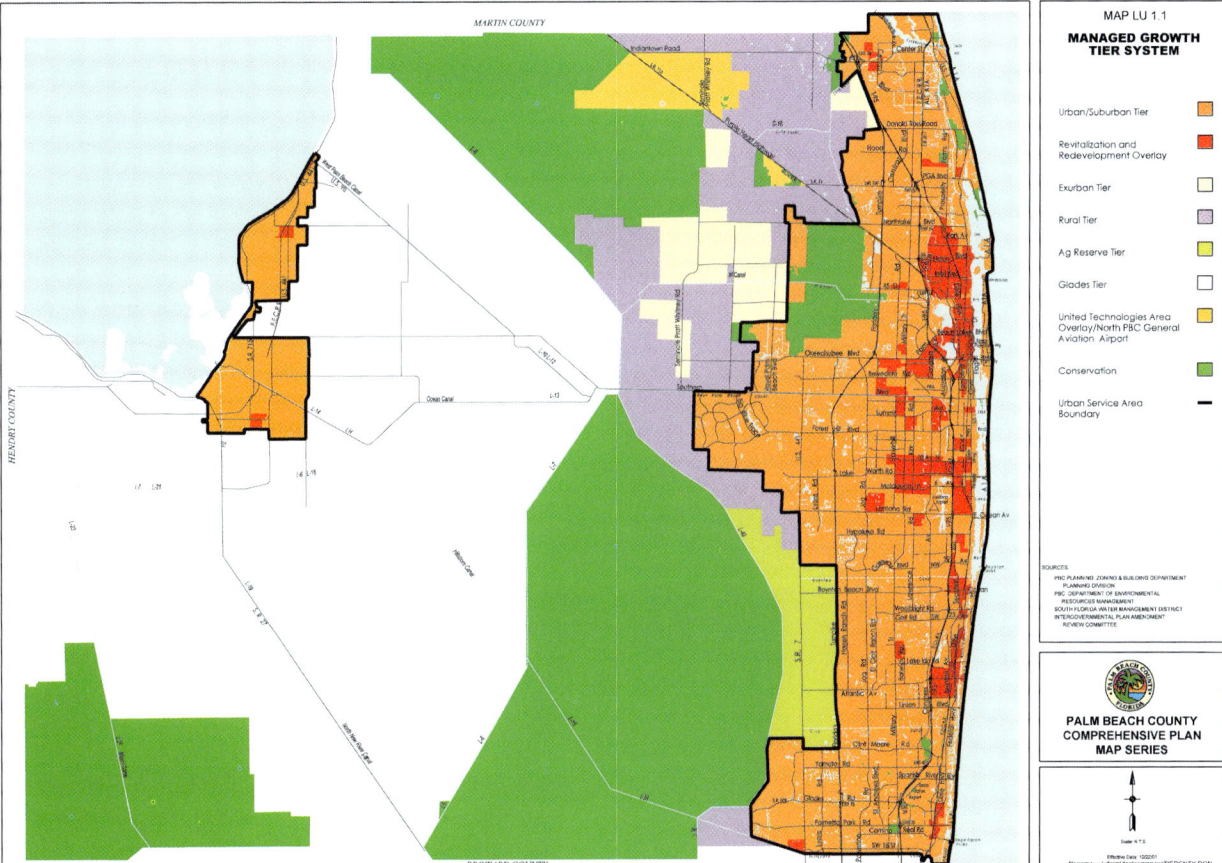

The MGTS and amended county plan provide a framework for managing three of the county's key growth-related risks (Palm Beach County 2003):

- First, to prevent the potential decay of older coastal areas, the county directed the bulk of its anticipated population growth, services, and employment to support redevelopment of these areas.

- Second, to reduce the loss of open space, critical environmental habitat, and agricultural businesses, the county reduced permissible development densities in several tiers and also limited nonresidential uses. The county also purchased farms and environmentally sensitive lands with municipal bonds and designated a 20,000-acre agricultural reserve with development rights transfers.

- Finally, to overcome the political instability seen in previous planning efforts, the county promoted good multijurisdictional participation and collaboration throughout the planning process to strengthen support.

Since its adoption in 1999, the county has continued to refine the MGTS and has also faced several challenges. In 2000, the county began work on a sector plan that would allow for limited future development in the rural and exurban tiers of the MGTS but also maintain the natural environment, rural character, and lifestyle choices in rural and semi-rural areas of the county. The sector plan is an optional process under Florida's state planning regulations. Since the county began its sector planning in 2000, the process has been controversial with large landowners in the affected areas, and increasing development pressures and breakdowns in communications have jeopardized the adoption and implementation of the plan (Hoyos 2004). In 2003, the county also incorporated the MGTS into its new Unified Land Development Code (ULDC), which went into effect in January 2004. Integrating the MGTS into the ULDC makes the county's land uses "tier-oriented," and the same set of land-use regulations are no longer applied countywide. County staff feels that the MGTS's success will depend, in part, upon the effectiveness of the county's new ULDC implementation.

In 2003, a state-mandated evaluation (Evaluation and Appraisal Report (EAR)) of the county's comprehensive plan concluded that the MGTS was working. It also found that it was still too soon to know whether the sector planning effort and the new ULDC will effectively reduce risks to the county's rural lifestyle and also promote long-term sustainability in these areas. The EAR focused on six issues and documented public input on each issue. (For more information on the EAR, please go to www.pbcgov.com/pzb/ and follow the links.)

In 2003, The Scripps Research Institute (TSRI) selected Palm Beach County as the future location of its East Coast operations, which posed one of the first real challenges to the county's MGTS. TSRI is the world's largest biotechnology research organization, and its East Coast campus will rival the Research Triangle in North Carolina and similar research centers in Europe. TSRI's location in Palm Beach County would have many fiscal and economic benefits for the county and South Florida; it would also strengthen and expand the county's reputation. TSRI would effectively be a new town development, complete with universities, schools, workforce housing, and a cluster of biotech-related industries.

The State of Florida and Palm Beach County put together a $500 million package to win TSRI, offering to fund construction and infrastructure and assuring the project's opening by mid-2006. But TSRI's preferred location is in the county's rural tier outside the Urban Service Boundary (USB) and the urban/suburban tier. The north-central county location is at odds with the county's MGTS and sector plan process, which have aimed to protect rural tier areas, such as the TSRI proposed site—an orange grove west of Palm Beach Gardens. Planning studies had also previously concluded that the county's projected growth to the year 2025 could be absorbed without opening rural lands to development (Hoyos 2004).

After months of heated debates and negotiations, Palm Beach County commissioners finally approved TSRI's proposed location in October 2004 and agreed to initiate construction. But their approval was conditional. Commissioners subtracted 2 million square feet off TSRI plans, concluding that there was ample additional space for biotech companies in nearby industrial and commercial zoned lands (Mertz 2004). The county estimates there is more than 5 million square feet of unused industrial space nearby.

Land speculation is underway on lands surrounding the TSRI site. Large landowners have proposed high-density urban development, and nearby cities are trying to anticipate development plans with annexations. TSRI has also proposed several risk mitigations as part of its design. It proposed to be a self-contained, walkable new town with mixed-use development, schools, affordable housing, work-live units, electric vehicles, and other elements to minimize traffic generation and preserve the Everglades (Hoyos 2004). Nonetheless, environmentalists and opponents of suburban sprawl have vowed to fight the plan, and lawsuits are expected, with the potential to freeze the project (Mertz 2004).

A second current challenge to the MGTS involves the Glades tier. The Glades tier comprises a vast agricultural area (more than 500,000 acres) dedicated to sugarcane cultivation in the western reaches of Palm Beach County. This area is part of the northern Everglades ecosystem and locally referred to as the Everglades Agricultural Area (EAA). The EAA is a critical component of the $12 billion federal and state Comprehensive Everglades Restoration Program (CERP). Development pressures are emerging on the eastern portion of this tier, near the small towns around Lake Okeechobee. Sugarcane farmers have made several failed attempts to change zoning that would allow for suburban development. But the county insists on holding the urban service boundary east of the sugarcane fields and continues to prohibit non-farming-related residential development in the EAA.

The county has also amended the development code to protect the EAA and tailored plan policies to create a "Glades Protection Tier," which protects the area from the encroachment of urban and suburban development. It also has created a "Glades Communities Tier" to accommodate redevelopment in some of the depressed cities along Lake Okeechobee. Palm Beach County commissioners have also directed staff to conduct an areawide comprehensive evaluation and needs assessment of the EAA to identify Everglades restoration priorities.

It has taken both the state of Florida and Palm Beach County several tries to build coordinated planning for growth management that addresses the risks inherent in an area under extreme growth pressures. On the basis of the most recent evaluation of the county's efforts, it appears that the MGTS is a well-functioning system with sufficient flexibility, and the county staff is committed to the principles of the system and its objectives to manage growth-related risks in a way that balances economic development, sustainability, and the protection of one of the nation's most prized environmental assets, the Everglades.

CALVERT COUNTY, MARYLAND: REACTING TO SMART GROWTH INCENTIVES

Calvert County, like many areas of Maryland, developed at a rapid pace in the 1980s and 1990s. Its prime location drew scores of new residents: it lies within commuting distance of the Washington, D.C., and Baltimore metro areas. It also has considerable natural assets, bordering the Chesapeake Bay and crossed by the Patuxent River. The county's population nearly doubled to 75,000 in less than two decades (Irwin and Bockstael 2002). Not surprisingly, as the population grew and more houses were built in the county, its character began to change.

By the 1990s, the county was exhibiting many of the negative signs of urban sprawl seen in communities around the country. The county led the state in the amount of agricultural and forested land being converted to residential use (Calvert County Planning Commission 1997). The number of commuters on county roads was growing rapidly, with the average

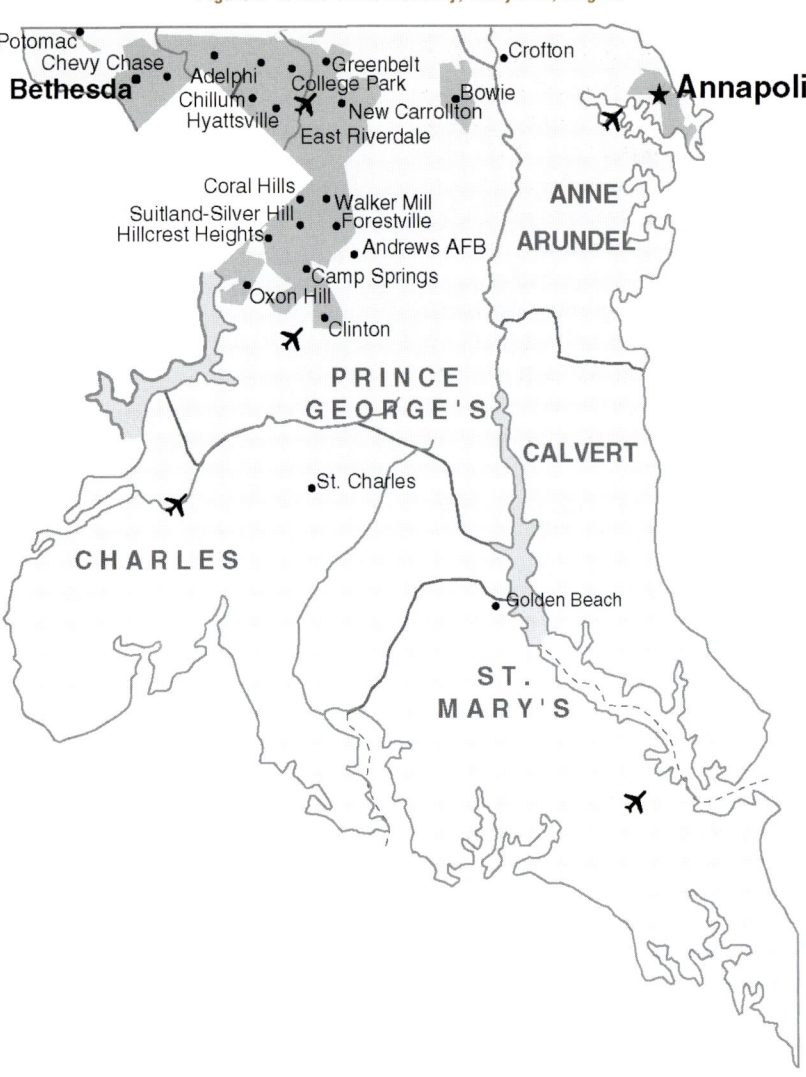

Figure 3-4. The Calvert County, Maryland, Region

commute drive time nearing 40 minutes (Guzzeau 2002). These changes were occurring despite a central focus since 1967 in successive county comprehensive plans on retaining the rural character of the county and slowing growth. Previous planning efforts to limit growth, including large-lot zoning, farmland preservation programs, development clustering requirements, and adequate public facilities acts, proved counterproductive, too slow, or temporary in their effects. These changes placed at risk the county's environment, traditional livelihoods (e.g., farming and fishing), and quality of life. They also threatened the county's fiscal health. As stated by Maryland's governor, "Every new classroom costs $90,000. Every mile of new sewer line costs roughly $200,000. And every single-lane mile of new road costs at least $4 million" (Cohen 2002).

The changing face of Maryland's countryside attracted little attention for decades. Public concern was not widely heard until evidence surfaced in the early 1990s that changing land-use patterns were causing accelerating decline of the Chesapeake Bay (Glendening 2004). The public and lawmakers started to take notice of sprawl, and several strategies were promoted to guide growth into denser, "smarter" patterns across the state. A state commission proposed strict mandates and oversight at the state level for all land-use decisions, but this approach was firmly opposed by many different interest groups and never made it out of legislative committee. A concerned governor, Parris Glendening, worked with citizen and stakeholder groups to develop an innovative, incentive-based approach to better manage growth in the state. Before designing the new approach, the governor insisted it include flexibility and local control (Cohen 2002).

The Smart Growth Areas Act of 1997

In 1997, the Smart Growth and Neighborhood Conservation Act (also referred to as the Smart Growth Areas Act), Chapter 759 of Maryland laws of 1997, passed into law. This law was part of a suite of legislation focusing on encouraging smart growth, preserving rural character, creating jobs near housing, and safeguarding the environment. The act relied on incentives to encourage development in specific areas and discourage it in others rather than a more regulatory approach, like urban growth boundaries.

The key smart growth component of the act was the development of Priority Funding Areas (PFAs). The act stated that all state growth-related funding must be funneled only to PFAs, including funding for highways, sewer and water system construction, economic development assistance, and state leases or construction of office buildings. Communities also were required to make sure local infrastructure kept pace with development to qualify for growth-related funds. Two possible ways include assessing development impact fees or enforcing an Adequate Public Facilities Ordinance (APFO), which requires new development to be limited to the capacity of public services. The goal was to align state development incentives with smart growth principles (State of Maryland Office of Planning 1998).

The state designated specific areas as PFAs, including municipalities, land inside the Baltimore Beltway, state land within the Capital Beltway, and enterprise zones. Local governments were given the authority to designate additional PFAs, generally lands zoned for dense development and with existing or planned water and sewer systems (Maryland Office of Planning 1997).

Maryland's Smart Growth legislation did not pass effortlessly; it required considerable coalition building and personal attention from the governor. County officials, interpreting land-use reform as an erosion of their power, initially strongly opposed the program. Likewise, business and development interests equated Smart Growth with antigrowth and staunchly opposed early proposals. Governor Glendening found early support among municipalities, environmental groups, and community leaders, and used many public and private meetings, conferences, and the media to build support among a more diverse group. Further, he exerted political pressure on state lawmakers when developing the 1997 state budget to encourage them to vote for the Smart Growth suite of legislation (Glendening 2004).

Land-Use Changes in the County

Calvert County submitted its required map of PFAs to the Maryland Department of Planning by 1999, designating only existing communities as priority areas for future growth. In other words, undeveloped areas that were planned to receive water and/or sewer service in the future were not included in their PFA designations although they could have been and were, thus, specified by the county as ineligible for state subsidies (1000 Friends of Maryland and Chesapeake Bay Foundation 1999).

Since the law was passed, Calvert County has continued to grow at an amazing pace. Between 1990 and 2001, Calvert County saw the fastest population growth rate of any county in the state. Despite the new state incentives, much of this growth has been housed in new residences constructed outside of the county-designated PFAs. The State Department of Planning found that between 1998 and 2001, 42 percent of all new home construction in the county occurred in PFAs. This statistic is not encouraging considering that, between 1990 and 1997, 58 percent of new home construction occurred in these areas (Maryland Department of Planning 2003). Across the county, the percent of development occurring in PFAs has actually gone down since the Smart Growth Areas Act was passed. It will take many years before the impacts of the law can be accurately assessed, however, due to the time lag associated with changing development patterns.

The price of an average home is growing rapidly in Calvert County, up by 46 percent from 2000 to 2003 (Calvert County Department of Economic Development 2004). The county is attracting residents with means who often prefer the larger lots found in development outside PFAs. County officials have expressed concerns that limiting state incentives for affordable housing to PFA areas only will concentrate low-income residents in

Maryland's Smart Growth legislation did not pass effortlessly; it required considerable coalition building and personal attention from the governor.

town centers and depress property values. Reportedly, Calvert County reduced allowable densities in some areas by half to address citizens' concerns on this issue (Cohen 2002).

In other locations in the county, local governments seeking to avoid growth have used provisions of the Smart Growth Areas Act to remove themselves from PFA zones. For example, the town of Dunkirk voted not to approve plans to develop water and sewer systems in the community. This move did not, however, prevent a new shopping center from being constructed; instead, new development relies on septic systems, which have environmental risks associated with their overconcentration.

Despite the sobering sprawl statistics in Calvert County, it is actually faring better than other Maryland counties with similar characteristics. Other newly developing suburban counties within striking distance of the state's major metropolitan areas have been consuming an even higher percentage of acres outside of PFAs with new homes, such as nearby Queen Anne and Saint Mary Counties.

One obvious weakness of the act in limiting sprawl is that it does not prevent private or local government funding of infrastructure in non-PFA areas. Political realities in Maryland, however, make it unlikely any law limiting local government's ability to build or approve infrastructure where it desires would have passed the legislature. This weakness has been exacerbated by state budget problems. Currently, the state is unable to cover all of the identified capital and infrastructure needs of local governments it normally would. A 1998 survey by the Maryland Department of Planning found a funding gap at the state level for local infrastructure of more than $9 billion over a six-year period and significantly more over longer periods. This necessitates developer-funded infrastructure, which is more likely to go to currently undeveloped areas outside of defined PFA zones because of the ease of construction (Cohen 2002).

The ability of the Smart Growth Act to survive political change and the loss of its personal champion—Governor Glendening—is now being tested. In 2003, Robert Ehrlich Jr. was elected governor of Maryland. Early signs indicate that many of the smart growth measures will continue to be supported, although different language is being used by the new administration. It is clear, however, that smart growth is not the new governor's top priority, and there is likely to be less personal involvement in making sure large development projects adhere to smart growth principles. The state is currently facing a difficult economic period, and the staff of the state Smart Growth Office was recently reshuffled.

Reactions in Calvert County to the state incentives to limit sprawl have been mixed. Many steps have been taken to encourage smart growth, such as limiting PFAs to already developed areas. Other actions, at both the county and municipal level, show residents continue to desire large-lot lifestyles and distrust state intervention in land-use decisions. Growth trends in the county since the passage of the law in 1997 indicate that the state's incentives have not yet adequately counterbalanced economic and social pressures for sprawl. But awareness of the negative impacts of sprawling growth seems to be on the rise in Calvert County and elsewhere. Only time will tell whether this program will have a lasting impact on shaping the state's growth.

SAINT PAUL, MINNESOTA: REGIONAL TAX-BASE SHARING

Like every major metropolitan area, the Twin Cities metro region in Minnesota has great disparities in wealth among its municipalities. In the 1960s and 1970s, the city of Saint Paul was representative of the region's older urban centers, with high and growing concentrations of poor residents, declining industries, and older city infrastructure. Its population declined by 1.1 percent in the 1960s, then by 12.8 percent in the 1970s. From a base of 313,411 in 1960, it had lost more than 43,000 residents in two decades. Still, compared to some northern cities, the decline was modest; Detroit, Cleveland, and Pittsburgh all lost more than a quarter of their populations during the same period. Since the 1980 census, Saint Paul has experienced a slow but steady growth in its population. Meanwhile, however, the suburbs ringing the Minneapolis/Saint Paul metro area were developing rapidly, drawing new businesses and attracting well-off residents who formerly made urban centers like Saint Paul their home. Regionally, the disparities between wealthy communities and poor ones were intensifying.

Saint Paul faced a problem common to many older urban areas surrounded by recently developed suburbs: tax revenues in the region were mismatched with need. Newer communities located outside of traditional city cores generally had more space, newer infrastructure, and low tax rates to attract new, lucrative development. Older communities, like Saint Paul, had outdated infrastructure in need of expensive maintenance and blocks crowded with older buildings reflecting needs from past generations. Former industrial areas in the city were left as polluted brownfields, inhibiting redevelopment of these sites by raising costs and legal concerns.

As new businesses decided to locate in developing suburbs, the revenues they brought increased disparities between new and old communities, provided funds for the new communities to improve their already superior services, and boosted incentives for additional new development to locate in these new communities. Communities with the worst social problems and highest need for services were seeing ever lower tax-bases; those with few social problems continued to grow their tax revenues. Residents with means fled older communities to areas with better services and lower property taxes, fueling a cycle of sprawl and economic separation.

In the 1960s, examples began to surface of communities making development decisions that benefited their own revenue streams but harmed the region as a whole. For example, a large power plant was built along the Saint Croix River in a location many people in the region hoped could be preserved as a waterfront park. The municipality where the plant was located claimed it needed the increased tax base and had no responsibility to develop leisure sites for the region without compensation (Jenni 2001). Further, people noted local jurisdictions competing for business development. Cities had incentives to offer lower tax rates, provide subsidies, build infrastructure, or reduce environmental and other standards to encourage a business to locate within their boundaries. In the end, lower tax revenues

Residents with means fled older communities to areas with better services and lower property taxes, fueling a cycle of sprawl and economic separation.

and degrading development standards hurt the entire region, even when businesses had already decided to locate in the region before the competition among jurisdictions began.

Despite clear interdependencies between neighboring communities, taxes in the Twin Cities region, as in most parts of the country, were collected individually by each jurisdiction. Development patterns influence tax income in communities, and individual tax collection programs encourage each community to focus on its own revenue needs rather than promoting development patterns to benefit all nearby communities. Leading up to the 1970s, lawmakers in the Twin Cities region of Minnesota began to observe and recognize that these undesirable development patterns were driven by increased economic disparities among and competition between local jurisdictions. The state legislature crafted an innovative program to share some tax revenues regionally in an effort to benefit all communities in the area and reverse some of these trends.

The Twin Cities Fiscal Disparities Plan

In 1971, the Minnesota legislature passed the Charles R. Weaver Metropolitan Revenue Distribution Act, commonly referred to as the Twin Cities fiscal disparities program, which is a regional tax-base sharing scheme. The plan mandated that taxes generated on commercial and industrial properties after 1971 should be shared among all municipalities in the region. Specifically, the total net change in net tax capacity since 1971 is shared, including taxes generated by post-1971 development, inflation, revaluation, appreciation, demolition, and depreciation (Hinze and Baker 2000). Sixty percent of tax revenues from such development go to the local jurisdiction, and the remaining 40 percent is put in a regional pool. A formula that considers factors such as population and fiscal capacity determines how the regional pool of tax funds should be shared. This program distributes tax revenues from communities with high levels of post-1971 industrial and commercial tax-base growth to communities that have had low levels of such growth.

The key goal of the program is to increase the ability of communities with low levels of commercial development to maintain their city services and reduce the increase in economic differences between older and newer communities. In the words of the former associate director of the Minnesota Citizens League, Paul Gilje, the program acts as a "good insurance policy. Nobody knows where the new growth is going to be, but under this plan, you're going to get a piece of it. This is the premium you have to pay" (Toland 2004).

This groundbreaking scheme has been in place for more than 30 years. There are 187 municipalities in the Twin Cities area now participating in the program. In 2004, $252 million went into the regional tax-base sharing pool. This represents about 10 percent of the total regional tax base and 30 percent of the regional commercial and industrial tax base. Forty-seven communities were net contributors to the fund; 140 communities were net receivers. Saint Paul was the largest recipient of funds in 2004, as in previous years, with $13.4 million flowing into the city from this program (Doboer 2004), although this figure does not subtract the city's own contribution to the pool from its own commercial/industrial tax base. On a per capita basis, however, several suburbs actually were larger recipients than Saint Paul. It is not unusual in many metropolitan areas for some smaller inner-ring suburbs to be more economically challenged than their central cities, a point stressed by former State Senator Myron Orfield, a long-time champion of the program (Orfield 1997, 2002).

Tax-base sharing was a controversial and divisive idea from the moment it was introduced. Its passage in the 1970s is attributed to detailed economic analyses showing that a majority of jurisdictions, including Saint Paul, would benefit from the program. Thus, a majority of legislators supported the law. Prior to these analyses being widely publicized, the program was viewed by most cities as threatening their local control or as a "communist" plot. Legislators from net contributor communities, such as wealthy suburbs, strongly opposed the law (Orfield 1996). After its passage, they challenged the law in court up to the Minnesota Supreme Court, where it was upheld.

Impacts on Land Use

Saint Paul has changed significantly since the 1970s and is today a thriving example of urban renewal. Poverty in the city continued to grow throughout the 1970s and 1980s, but saw a sharp turnaround in the 1990s. By the 2000 census, the percent of people living in poverty in the city dropped by nearly 10 percent from the previous decade (Metropolitan Council 2004). At the same time, Saint Paul was undertaking ambitious renewal projects, including revitalizing its waterfront, renovating parks and infrastructure, and attracting new, diverse businesses.

Clearly the city has benefited from the fiscal disparities program. The Minnesota Department of House Research estimates that the average homeowner in Saint Paul paid nearly 13 percent less in property taxes and the average commercial-industrial property paid 11.5 percent less in taxes than would be the case if the program were abolished (Hinze and Baker 2000). Saint Paul's financial services director says the city would need to raise taxes significantly or reduce expenditures by millions of dollars if the program did not exist (Toland 2004). The regionally generated funds play a role in the city's recent successes revitalizing neighborhoods, industry, and infrastructure.

Besides the fiscal disparities program, new waves of immigration, including large populations of Hmong and Somali people, also played a part in Saint Paul's revitalization, as did immigration patterns in many other central cities in the 1980s and 1990s. In addition, a revival of interest in urban living in the 1990s propped up urban populations in a number of central cities, including both of the Twin Cities. Saint Paul is not unique in its reductions in poverty: poverty in central cities has been dropping dramatically in many parts of the country since the 1990s, particularly in the Midwest (Jargowsky 2003). Saint Paul is, however, one of the few midwestern cities that saw both an increase in population and a decrease in poverty during this time. While the fiscal disparities program cannot be conclusively linked to the city's recent positive trends, it is notable that Saint Paul received the greatest income from the program in the 1990s (Hinze and Baker 2000).

Monitoring the Program's Success

There have been surprisingly few changes to the fiscal disparities law since it was passed more than 30 years ago. Only two minor adjustments have been made. One allows the community that constructed the Mall of America (the country's largest mall) to adjust its contributions until bonds covering highway improvements to the site are paid off. The other sends a limited amount of funds to an affordable housing incentive program operated by the Metropolitan Council (Hinze and Baker 2000). The lack of change to the law has more to do with the politics of changing the program than its perfection. The law remains firmly unpopular among wealthy

Tax-base sharing was a controversial and divisive idea from the moment it was introduced.

communities that contribute each year, and every few years, legislators representing those areas introduce bills to change or abolish the program, so far unsuccessfully (Orfield 1996).

Over the past decades, many people have noted aspects of the law that do not support its original goals. The program's focus only on commercial and industrial tax revenues means that wealthy residential communities with low levels of commercial development receive payments from the program despite their lack of need. Inequalities among communities that existed prior to 1971 remain unaddressed by the program since it only spreads tax-base growth after that date.

Competition between communities for big projects continues even though the fiscal disparities program does serve to limit the net gain of one municipality over another when it succeeds in attracting a new commercial or industrial facility others also want. Only if 100 percent of this tax base were shared would the competition become pointless and cease. In Saint Paul, only 25 percent of such a new facility's taxable value would enter the regional pool because the program uses a citywide rather than property-specific percentage in its calculations. It has also been suggested the program may actually fuel sprawl in the region's outermost suburbs by subsidizing the infrastructure required for large-lot residential development (Doboer 2004). Addressing any of these concerns has proved difficult. In 1995, the state House and Senate passed a law to expand the tax-base-sharing program to include revenues from high-end residential properties. This change was vetoed by the governor and did not go into effect.

The Twin Cities' tax-base sharing scheme continues to be a revolutionary program to spread the risks associated with development patterns across the entire region. While not perfect, it is clear the program has led to a regional perspective on development and reductions in economic differences between communities. This holistic risk management program could not have been undertaken by any one city: it required regional cooperation.

While not perfect, it is clear the program has led to a regional perspective on development and reductions in economic differences between communities.

CHAPTER 4

Putting It All Together: Establishing a Risk-Management-Based Approach to Planning in Your Community

A page was turned in all our lives on September 11. Let's not turn the page back and relive the same mistakes. The time is ripe for new definitions and new approaches to bring forth the vision for a better future that exists in all of our minds. —MICHAEL KUO, IMAGINE NEW YORK, 2004

So far, we have defined a suite of risks that may affect communities, and we have also examined a framework for managing risk as well as some real-world examples. Now it is time to put it all together and address why local planners are ideal risk managers and how they can effectively launch these efforts.

WHY LOCAL IMPLEMENTATION IS BEST

Local government is the only place that can sensibly implement risk-based land-use management. Land-use decisions happen at the local level, and risk assessment is a bottom-up, multistakeholder, interdisciplinary practice—not a top-down authoritarian practice. Risk management efficiently buffers a community from impacts to its physical structures, social and cultural fabric, economic vitality, and environmental assets. By incorporating risk management into land-use planning, the benefits that accrue to communities through good urban design and land-use practice are likely to last through time. Therefore, incorporating the structured approach of risk management into ongoing planning processes is an easy fit for many jurisdictions.

Since there is no "one size fits all" solution to land-use planning, it needs the local perspective to be properly tailored. Each community stands unique in its population, cultural composition, and planning challenges. States, like Florida, Maryland, and California, can set up mandates and policy frameworks, but there are countless examples of the same mandates being implemented much less successfully in each of these states and elsewhere. Mandates typically filter down to local levels very differently. "Planning mandates are especially helpful because they stimulate analyses of the extent of historical losses and assessments of future risks" (Nelson and French 2002). The communities selected for our case studies illustrate how mandates and similar planning frameworks can be used to achieve a greater objective and to address risk factors.

Many local regulatory tools have been created from model guidelines and may not necessarily integrate well with the community's goals or tests for consistency. Rigid planning approaches provide little flexibility and require amendment after amendment. Many planning tools obligate local agencies to address only a particular set of issues and lack a comprehensive view. Furthermore, they often lack specific guidance for agencies to use in resolving the issues (May and Williams 1986). If planners stick to traditional risk review processes based solely on regulatory compliance, the bigger questions may not be asked, the broadest public interest will not be addressed, and the community's subtle evolutionary processes will be missed. Mandated approaches typically emphasize identification and mitigation of specific negative impacts without addressing other risks and inevitably pass those risks to others. The risk management framework outlined in this report will help overcome current process limitations that assess impacts only. It will also ensure a greater chance of success in meeting the community's unique needs and cultivating its opportunities.

By allowing profit, we have traditionally acknowledged the major financial risks private land developers take in buying land and making necessary plans, investments, and improvements (Beatley 1994). But, today, many public agencies are struggling with the costly effects of the continued growth and sprawl for which they have assumed responsibility. For example, the public costs of supporting water and sewer services to single-family residential development patterns have increased significantly as lot sizes increase and development is more dispersed (Speir and Stephenson 2002). As we have seen in Maryland and Florida, smart growth initiatives and other political tools are challenging communities to alter their paradigms of land-use planning. Yet these alterations require considerable time and effort, and the path for considering alternative approaches is riddled with uncertainty.

A risk-based framework for land-use planning offers communities a rational means for understanding and managing the inevitable change. It also provides a means for addressing the financial risk exposure in

> *If planners stick to traditional risk review processes based solely on regulatory compliance, the bigger questions may not be asked, the broadest public interest will not be addressed, and the community's subtle evolutionary processes will be missed.*

land-use decision making and the approval of public and private development projects. It can help address risk disparities, as we saw in the Twin Cities example. We should acknowledge that deficit spending at the federal level and in many states is possible, likely to continue, and may even increase in years to come. Coupling this situation with growing public safety demands and concerns about better financial management at the local level, the financial benefits and needs for better risk-based land-use planning approaches increase substantially.

USING THE LAND-USE PLANNING FRAMEWORK FOR IMPLEMENTATION

There are two key windows of opportunity for implementing risk management approaches. The first is at the strategic level, with a community's next comprehensive plan or other broad planning update effort. Using the concepts described in this report, this effort can be expanded to holistically and systematically assess the various hazards or triggering events that each community may face, to evaluate various vulnerable exposures, and to determine risk thresholds and risk decision options. With a new general plan in place, there are then subsequent opportunities to revise various tactical procedures, like zoning and subdivision regulations, building codes, and other elements of the planners' tool kit, to be consistent with the risk decision framework incorporated into the new plan. To be effective, the process should include the following actions:

- Develop the necessary tools to identify and assess risks and develop a risk management matrix for your community. This may include conducting parcel-specific assessments of land-uses and structures, inventorying social and historical resources and risks, and undertaking risk mapping through a geographic information system (GIS).

- Conduct a survey or a citizen participation process to determine your community's risk thresholds, and prioritize these risks for action.

- Evaluate risk decision options for priority risks and develop an overall risk management strategy. Citizen participation may be useful to achieve consensus on the decisions and overall strategy.

- Incorporate the strategy into your community planning process. Implement the strategy through neighborhood or more specific risk management plans or action plans for priority risks.

- And finally, implement tactical operations for managing risks and monitoring progress. This needs to be bottom up, starting at the project review level and including potential subdivision regulation changes and design review procedures.

If the comprehensive plan update window is not going to open in your community any time soon, the other key opportunity window is development review.

If the comprehensive plan update window is not going to open in your community any time soon, the other key opportunity window is development review. A risk management approach to development review will incorporate a larger eye to consider the temporal and contextual aspects of a project. Not only can it help to evaluate how a specific project might evolve through time, but it can also help consider how the surrounding neighborhood and entire community may change, and how the project will fit into that setting during its life cycle. Some essential risk considerations in project review include the following:

- What hazards/triggering events potentially affect the project?
- Does the project have characteristics that increase risks?
- What is the expected life of the project?

- How will its business model be sustained over that project life?
- What are the risks that this model will not be sustainable?
- How will demographics and cultural profiles change through time?
- What does it mean to the economic sustainability proposed for the project?
- For what risks are government agencies/departments each responsible?
- What risks are and are not acceptable and what risk management options are available?
- Who should be involved from other departments, sectors, or other communities in the risk review and project approval process?
- What are the conditions for project denial or approval?
- What risk management actions are to be implemented and monitored?

PLANNERS ARE IDEALLY SITUATED TO DO RISK MANAGEMENT

Planners are the right people to implement risk-based land-use planning frameworks because they have access to both the strategic and tactical tools for building safe, attractive, and healthy communities to serve all residents. Understanding and managing risks is a natural fit with these objectives. Planners were key players in all four case studies we featured in Chapter 3.

With the shifting economic and sociodemographic realities of today, state and local governments are being challenged to move beyond their traditional role as regulators and into a new role as collaborators, capacity builders, and creators of new opportunity. Communities are developing more collaborative approaches that will attract and retain business and industry. Planners are critical members of such collaborative efforts: they are key to creating a vision for their community's changing needs and helping stakeholders to understand the positive and negative risks of the decisions made. Their roles in decision making mean we are predisposed to be the facilitators and architects of new approaches. But planners do not simply provide every good and service requested; they must also regulate the actions of governments, developers, and residents so as to prevent, for example, building on wetlands or the elimination of affordable housing (Krumholz 2001).

PLANNERS ALSO NEED TO SEEK COLLABORATION AND SUPPORT

Implementing a different approach to decision making requires support from a broad range of community members. Risk management needs a leader, and it is also needs internal champions to develop incentives, search out external resources, and get training when necessary.

First and foremost, organizational support is essential and must be built from the start. Champions must be cultivated, and key department staff and city council members must be supportive and help put it all together. It will also be helpful to raise community awareness and possibly recruit private developers and other key stakeholders into the process. In doing so, remember to emphasize the benefits of collaboration, increased organizational capacity, and enhanced communications. Innovative community outreach, both traditional and nontraditional, gains importance when it effectively ensures quality of life for the widest range of community members. Collaboration is increasingly "advocated as a more effective approach to planning and management, especially for complex topics" (Margerum 2002). With communication, look to make the process transparent, especially with the community

Planners are the right people to implement risk-based land-use planning frameworks because they have access to both the strategic and tactical tools....

and key stakeholders, and don't be afraid to identify and discuss risks and their impacts. A cross-cultural communication process is a critical two-way process that breaks through cultural divides. Ten steps can lead toward more effective collaborative outreach:

1. Involve community stakeholders and champions
2. Customize outreach for audiences—use sociocultural indicators
3. Craft effective strategic approaches, tools, and messages in a campaign-styled approach
4. Be creative and take risks
5. Create ownership by individual "communities within the community"
6. Incorporate local perspectives
7. Create two-way communication opportunities
8. Aggressively involve community leaders
9. Speak with one voice on message issues
10. Evaluate and measure performance of outreach

Incentives for developers can also help institutionalize a risk management approach and encourage community leaders and developers to be involved. Incentives could take the form of reductions in infrastructure fees and expedited permit review. As another option, local property tax systems might be modified to reflect the risk management actions taken. Much as farmers get reduced property tax assessments, land where risk is mitigated could be taxed at lower rates to reflect the value of the public service provided by them.

Training and expert resources are also helpful, especially since risk management is not yet a standard part of most planning school curricula. The Public Entity Risk Institute (PERI), established in 1996, serves public, private, and nonprofit organizations with dynamic, forward-thinking resources for the practical enhancement of risk management. PERI provides synergy among existing programs and organizations and serves as a catalyst in the risk management field and a vehicle for allocating greater resources to key needs in risk management. With its growing array of programs and projects, along with its grant funding, PERI is focused on:

- supporting the development and delivery of education and training on all aspects of risk management for public, nonprofit, and small business entities;
- serving as a resource center and clearinghouse for all areas of risk management;
- building a national database of loss information to help public officials improve the performance of their risk programs;
- developing comparative performance measurement and best practices; and
- operating an innovative, forward-looking grants and research program in risk management, environmental impairment liability, and disaster management.

In February 2003, PERI joined forces with the Public Risk Management Association (PRIMA) and the Nonprofit Risk Management Center (NRMC) to launch the Risk Management Resource Center (RMRC; www.eriskcenter.org).

BART OVERCOMES FEARS OF COMMUNICATING RISK

In November 2002, San Francisco Bay Area voters rejected a measure that would have allowed the Bay Area Rapid Transit District (BART) to issue up to $1.05 billion in bonds to perform seismic upgrades of BART facilities. The measure's passage required a two-thirds majority in three counties, but it passed in one, missed by one-tenth of a point in another, and was firmly rejected by voters in the third (Vorderbrueggen 2004). Some BART managers feared ridership would decrease if the system's risks were more fully disclosed, and their campaign communications were criticized as being muddled, using scare tactics, and not emphasizing the validity of seismic studies underpinning the measure.

BART learned from this experience and engaged in a much more transparent and collaborative campaign leading up to the measure's reconsideration on the November 2004 ballot. To start, BART enlisted the support of the region's earthquake safety experts and invited the media to walk through the system's seismically vulnerable tunnel running under San Francisco Bay. It also worked to secure a more diverse funding pool for the upgrades (Vorderbrueggen 2004). In doing so, BART's collaborative approach to address its capital risks is also addressing both its institutional and financial risks. In November 2004, two-thirds majorities in three San Francisco Bay Area counties finally voted to support the bond measure and the needed seismic upgrades.

RMRC provides information to help local governments, nonprofit organizations, and small businesses manage risks effectively and protect the people, property, assets, reputation, financial health, and services of these organizations. RMRC's online learning section includes free tutorials and courses on risk management. There are also free publications, risk management briefs, conference presentations, and a wealth of reference material available for review. Virtual symposia hosted by PERI on a variety of public risk-related topics are also available there, as well as at the PERI Web site (www.riskinstitute.org).

PERI has also teamed with the National Center for Small Communities (NCSC) and the Institute for Local Self Government (ILSG) to develop additional local risk management resources. PERI and the NCSC have developed a starter kit of tools and information as part of their "Community Leadership in a Risky World" initiative (PERI 2004). The starter kit is designed to help a small community initiate an effective risk management program and includes guidance on developing a risk management statement and a risk assessment template. The toolkit can be found on the Web sites of both PERI and the NCSC (www.smallcommunities.org). With support from PERI, the ILSG is developing a publication entitled *Reducing Land Use Liability: A Guide for Local Agencies* that will help local staff avoid land-use-related litigation. In particular, the guide is intended for small and midsize agencies without the funding or resources to hire risk management staff or outside counsel. The guide will be available on PERI's Web site.

GROWING AWARENESS OF RISK-BASED PLANNING

Since September 11, 2001, our sensitivity to risk has increased substantially. There is increasing recognition of national, regional, and local vulnerabilities to both man-made and natural hazards and risks. The tsunami disaster of December 2004 has certainly raised yet another specter of the horrendous damage to people, communities, culture, and economy as a result of vulnerability to risk. Communities across America and the world are reevaluating their exposures, strengthening public safety and awareness programs, and being vigilant in assessing and mitigating risks. They are learning more about who lives in their communities, as well as their needs and vulnerabilities. But the costs are not small. In a survey conducted by the U.S. Conference of Mayors, 93 mostly small and medium cities reported they expected to spend $122.5 million in the first year after September 11 in order to maintain heightened security (U.S. Conference of Mayors 2001). These increased costs covered the deployment of additional security personnel, short-term equipment needs, and public outreach and education efforts. More than $20 billion in federal aid has gone to the state of New York to respond to and recover from the September 11 terrorist attacks. Much of this funding came from FEMA and HUD. A great deal came very quickly as flexible block grants and included $4.5 billion to build a transit center linking the subway and commuter train systems around the former WTC site (Mammen 2005).

The formation of the Department of Homeland Security in 2002 formally linked together the counter-terrorism risk management training and education activities with natural hazards mitigation efforts of the Federal Emergency Management Agency (FEMA). This gave an increased scope and boost to community mitigation planning efforts already underway in compliance with the Disaster Mitigation Act (DMA 2000). The DMA is an excellent process for communities to use in leveraging a risk-based, land-use planning approach. Up to 7 percent of FEMA's Hazard Mitigation Grant Program funds are available to states to use in developing state, tribal, and local mitigation plans. Technical assistance grants are also available to communities to complete the plans.

Multigovernmental coordination and support for risk-based planning has continued with the adoption of the National Response Plan (NRP) and the National Incident Management System (NIMS) in 2003. NIMS provides a nationwide template for federal, state, tribal, and local governments; the private sector; and nongovernmental organizations to work together in preparing for and responding to all man-made and natural hazard incidents. NIMS establishes a standard system for all organizations to follow in managing an incident. The five functional areas in NIMS are: management, operations, planning, logistics, and finance/administration. FEMA has established a NIMS Web page at www.fema.gov/nims/ to provide emergency managers with tools and resources to implement NIMS. While many implementation challenges still lie ahead, NIMS is the first truly comprehensive and integrated, multiorganizational planning and response system in U.S. The NIMS system isn't just for emergency responders. It has also been proven to be effective in managing the many planning- and land-use-related actions local agencies must take in repairing and reconstructing following disasters (Johnson 1999).

Combined with bills such as the Intelligence Reform and Terrorism Prevention Act of 2004, passed into law in December 2004, these new federal initiatives can be used together to address longstanding risks as well as the newly growing and not-so-well-understood risks facing the country today. With the impact of globalization, planners at the national, state and local level as well as those also addressing development and economic issues outside U.S. borders are challenged to embrace new collaborative approaches, tools, and decision-making processes.

In Lower Manhattan, one of the most controversial and highly publicized land-use decisions of our times is progressing. Within days after the disaster, civic groups and countless volunteers organized to offer expertise in planning, design, and public participation to develop a long-term reconstruction strategy for the World Trade Center site and other affected parts of Lower Manhattan (Jacquemart 2002). In late November 2001, the state and city established the Lower Manhattan Development Corporation (LMDC) to develop the official plan for Lower Manhattan, in conjunction with the Port Authority (owner of the 16-acre site). Formal planning for redevelopment of the site began in 2002 and public input into the planning called for recognition of the former tower footprints as a memorial, a reduction of commercial space at the former site, and a restoration of the site's prominence in the Lower Manhattan skyline (LMDC 2003).

In early 2002, Imagine New York (INY) was conceived by a group of planners to help ensure that there was meaningful public participation and buy-in for the rebuilding process (INY 2004). While the LMDC was selecting consultants and starting its preliminary design work, INY conducted 257 workshops across the tri-state region and collected more than 19,000 ideas, which it analyzed and consolidated into 49 vision statements about the site, city, and region. In recognition of its efforts, APA gave INY the 2003 American Vision Award (Krasnow 2003). As LMDC has continued its planning and implementation, INY has also continued its public participation efforts, soliciting input on LMDC's preliminary plans in December 2002, the eight design finalists for the WTC memorial in November 2003, and many other LMDC planning studies and efforts (LMDC 2004; INY 2004).

But even with extensive public input, plans for the WTC redevelopment remain controversial. The final plans will still result in very dense, largely commercial-based redevelopment of the site. Infrastructure and transportation plans have focused on much-needed system upgrades

With the impact of globalization, planners at the national, state and local level as well as those also addressing development and economic issues outside U.S. borders are challenged to embrace new collaborative approaches, tools, and decision-making processes.

and enhancements, but they will also be densely interlinked through the redevelopment area, and the region's heavy dependence upon this site's functionality will continue. While the future reconstruction will not be risk-free, the various civic groups and responsible planning agencies did facilitate a robust public involvement process in the World Trade Center redevelopment. In doing so, they also raised awareness and promoted thoughtful dialogue about a range of risks and the land-use decisions being made. The process itself is a living memorial to the spirit of democracy and the resolve to move forward, a bit more wary of the risks we now know we face but a lot wiser about what we can do to manage them.

As with the redevelopment of the World Trade Center, the integration of information management and the overhaul of critical government functions, such as the emergency management and intelligence communities, also offer new opportunities for planners. Risk management, as a profession and a disciplinary practice, positions planners to more effectively deal with the complexities of a changing world. In this way, the unexpected becomes the anticipated, and the unforeseen is just one more decision point in a rich array of planning strategies.

List of References and Bibliography

American Planning Association/Federal Emergency Management Agency, 2001. *Planning for a Disaster-Resistant Community: A One-Day Workshop for City and County Planners, Planning Officials and Consultants*. June.

Applied Insurance Research (AIR). 2004. [Accessed January 10, 2005]. Available at www.air-worldwide.com.

Association of Environmental Professionals (AEP). 2000. "Environmental Mitigation Monitoring and Reporting Under the California Environmental Quality Act (CEQA)." [Accessed January 10, 2005]. Available at: www.califaep.org/legislation/mmrrp.html.

Beatley, Timothy. 1994. *Ethical Land-Use: Principles of Policy and Planning*. Baltimore, Md.: John Hopkins University Press.

Berkeley, City of. 2003. *General Plan*. [Accessed January 10, 2005]. Available at www.ci.berkeley.ca.us/planning/landuse/plans/generalPlan/Intro.html.

_____. 2004. *Disaster Mitigation Plan for the City of Berkeley*. Draft. [Accessed January 10, 2005]. Available at www.ci.berkeley.ca.us/manager/disastermitigation.html.

Bernstein, Peter L. 1996a. *Against the Gods: The Remarkable Story of Risk*. New York: John Wiley and Sons.

_____. 1996b. "The New Religion of Risk Management." *Harvard Business Review*, March-April, 47–50.

Burby, Raymond, and Peter J. May. 1997. "Chapter 4. Florida: Putting It All Together." *Making Governments Plan. State Experiments in Managing Land-Use*. Baltimore, Md.: John Hopkins University Press.

Burby, Raymond, Peter May, Emil Malizia, and Joyce Levine. 2000. "Building Code Enforcement Burdens and Central City Decline" *Journal of the American Planning Association* 66, no. 2 (spring): 143–161.

California, State of. [n.d.]. *Public Resources Code Section 21083 and Code of Regulations, Title 14, Section 15065*.

_____. [n.d.]. *Public Resources Code, Section 21081.6*.

_____. 1996. *Tracking CEQA Mitigation Measures Under AB 3180*. CEQA Technical Advice Series. Governor's Office of Planning and Research. 3rd ed. [Accessed January 10, 2005]. Available at http:ceres.ca.gov/topic/env_law/ceqa/more/tas/CEQA_Mitigation/CEQA_Mit.html.

Calvert County Department of Economic Development. 2004. "Calvert County 2003: State of the Economy." [Accessed January 10, 2005]. Available at www.ecalvert.com/StateoftheEconomy2004.pdf.

Calvert County Planning Commission, 1997. *Comprehensive Plan*. [Accessed January 10, 2005]. Available at www.co.cal.md.us/planning/compplan/compmain.htm.

Cohen, James R. 2002. "Maryland's 'Smart Growth': Using Incentives to Combat Sprawl." In *Urban Sprawl: Causes, Consequences and Policy Responses*, edited by Gregory D. Squires. Washington, D.C.: Urban Institute Press.

de Aragon, Fernando. 1996. "Palm Beach County, Florida: Why Regional Planning Failed." *Planner's Casebook*. American Institute of Certified Planners, American Planning Association, Chicago, Ill.: Spring.

DeGrove, John M. 1984. "Chapter 4. Florida: Harmonizing Growth and the Environment." *Land Growth & Politics*. Chicago, Ill.: Planners Press.

_____. 1992. "Chapter 2. Florida: A Second Try at Managing Massive Growth Pressures." In *Planning and Growth Management in the States*. Cambridge, Mass.: Lincoln Institute of Land Policy.

Deyle, Robert E., and Richard A. Smith. 1998. "Local Government Compliance with State Planning Mandates: The Effects of State Implementation in Florida." *Journal of the American Planning Association* 64, no. 4 (autumn): 457–469.

Deboer, Bob. 2004. "A New Look at Fiscal Disparities: Is it Subsidizing Development that Counters Regional Planning?" *Minnesota Journal* 21, no. 3 (March): 4–7. [Accessed February 2, 2005]. Available at www.citizensleague.net/html/mn_journal.html.

Earthquake Engineering Research Institute (EERI). 1997. "Insurance." *Earthquake Basics Brief No. 3*. Oakland, Calif.: EERI.

EQECAT. 2004. [Accessed January 10, 2005]. Available at www.eqecat.com.

Federal Emergency Management Agency (FEMA). 2001. *Understanding Your Risks: Identifying Hazards and Estimating Losses (FEMA 386–2)*. August.

_____. 2002. "Hazard Mitigation Planning and Hazard Mitigation Grant Program." *Federal Register* 67, no. 38.

_____. 2003. "Disaster-Resistant Jobs: Strategies for Community, Emergency, and Economic." *Risk Management Facilitator Guide*, p. 2–21.

Florida, State of, Department of Community Affairs. 1998. *The Local Mitigation Strategy: City and Counties Working Together to Build Disaster-Resistant Communities*. Tallahassee, Fla.: The Florida Department of Community Affairs.

Glendening, Parris. 2004. "Smart Politics." *The Environmental Forum*. January/February, 21–30.

Guzzeau, Gary J. 2002. *The Spatial Disconnect Between Resident and Job Locations in Maryland: Potential Demand for a Smart Growth Incentive Program* (master's paper, University of Maryland at College Park, Urban Studies and Planning Program). [Accessed January 10, 2005]. Available at www.caed.asu.edu/apa/proceedings03/S-GUZZ/s-guzz.htm.

Handmer, John, and Paul Thompson. 1996. *Economic Assessment of Disaster Mitigation: A Summary Guide*. Canberra, Australia: Centre for Resource and Environmental Studies, Australian National University.

Heinz Center, 2000. *The Hidden Costs of Coastal Hazards: Implications for Risk Assessment and Mitigation*. Washington D.C.: Island Press.

Hinze, Steve, and Karen Baker. 2000. *Minnesota's Fiscal Disparities Programs: Twin Cities Metropolitan Area and Iron Range*. [Available at January 10, 2005]. Available at www.house.leg.state.mn.us/hrd/pubs/fiscaldis.pdf.

Imagine New York (INY). 2004. [Accessed January 10, 2005]. Available at www.imagineny.org.

International Organization for Standardization (ISO). 2002. *Risk Management—Vocabulary—Guidelines for Use in Standards*. ISO/IEC Guide 73ISO. Geneva, Switzerland: Central Secretariat.

Irwin, Elena G., and Nancy E. Bockstael. 2002. "Managing Urban Sprawl: The Effects of Land-Use Externalities." Lincoln Institute of Land Policy: Cambridge, Mass.

Jacquemart, Georges. 2002. "Getting Lower Manhattan Moving Again." *Planning*, September, 4–9.

Jargowsky, Paul A. 2003. *Stunning Progress, Hidden Problems: The Dramatic Decline of Concentrated Poverty in the 1990s*. Washington D.C.: Center on Urban and Metropolitan Policy, The Brookings Institution.

Jenni, Phil. 2001. "It's a Miracle: Minnesota's Tax Base Sharing Law Survives for 30 Years." *Minnesota Journal*, The Citizens League, February 20, p 2.

Johnson, Laurie. 1999. *Empowering Local Governments in Disaster Recovery Management: Lessons from Watsonville and Oakland in Recovering from the 1989 Loma Prieta Earthquake and Other Recent Disasters*. Oakland, Calif.: Earthquake Engineering Research Institute.

Kloman, H. Felix. 1999. "Milestones: 1900 to 1999." *Risk Management Reports* 26, no. 12.

Knight, Frank. 1921. *Risk, Uncertainty, and Profit*. Boston, Mass.: Houghton Mifflin Company.

Krasnow, David. 2003. "Imagine New York." *Planning*, March, 16.

Krumholz, Norman. 2001. "The Three Most Exciting Trends In Planning." [Accessed January 10, 2005]. Available at www.planetizen.com.

Langdon, Philip. 2001. "The Long Road to Rebuilding Lower Manhattan." *Planning*, December, 4–11.

Lower Manhattan Development Corporation (LMDC). 2003. *Generic Environment Impact Statement*. [Accessed January 10, 2005]. Available at www.renewnyc.org/plan_des_dev/environmental_review.asp.

_____. 2004. [Accessed January 10, 2005]. Available at www.renewnyc.org.

Margerum, Richard D. 2002. "Evaluating Collaborative Planning: Implications from an Empirical Analysis of Growth Management." *Journal of the American Planning Association* 68, no. 2 (spring): 179–192.

Maryland, State of, Department of Legislative Services, Office of Policy Analysis. 2002. "Growth Management," *Spotlight*, July. [Accessed January 10, 2005]. Available at http:dls.state.md.us/side_pgs/2_policy_spotlight/policy_environment_natural_resources.html.

Maryland, State of, Department of Planning. 2003. "Data on Priority Funding Areas." [Available at January 10, 2005]. Available at www.mdp.state.md.us/msdc/PFA/pfa_idx.htm.

_____. 1998. *Managing Maryland's Growth, Models and Guidelines. Smart Growth: Municipal Implementation*. 2nd ed. Baltimore, Md.: Maryland Department of Planning.

_____. 1997. *Managing Maryland's Growth, Models and Guidelines. Smart Growth: Designating Priority Funding Areas*. Baltimore, Md.: Maryland Department of Planning.

Mammen, David. 2005. "Recovery: Lessons from New York and 9/11/01." Paper presented at the First International Conference on Urban Disaster Reduction, Kobe, Japan.

May, Peter, and Walter Williams. 1986. *Disaster Policy Implementation: Managing Programs Under Shared Governance*. New York: Plenum.

McClure, Diana L. 2002. "Are We Planning Safer Communities? Results of a National Survey of Community Planners." An invited comment in *Natural Hazards Observer* 26, no. 6: 1–3.

McHarg, Ian. 1969. *Design With Nature*. Garden City, N.Y.: John Wiley & Sons.

Meck, Stuart. 2000. "Current Topic Award: Growing Smart—Initiatives and Applications: Palm Beach County Managed Growth Program." *Planning*, April, 4–5.

Mertz, Cadence. 2004. "Pratt weighs options on developing property near Scripps." *South Florida Sun-Sentinel*, October 21.

Metro. 2004. Metro Regional Government, Portland Oregon. [Accessed January 10, 2005]. Available at www.metro-region.org.

Metropolitan Council. 2004. *Census 2000: Key Facts—Trouble at the Core Update*. [Accessed January 10, 2004]. Available at www.metrocouncil.org/Census/KeyFacts/Troubleat CoreUpdate.htm.

Mileti, Dennis S. 1999. *Disasters by Design, A Reassessment of Natural Hazards in the United States*. Washington, D.C.: Joseph Henry Press.

National Institute of Building Sciences (NIBS). 2004. HAZUS Multihazard Loss Estimation Methodology. [Accessed January 10, 2005]. Available at www.nibs.org/hazusweb/.

Nelson, Arthur C., and Steven P. French. 2002. "Plan Quality and Mitigating Damage from Natural Disasters: A Case Study of the Northridge Earthquake with Planning Policy Considerations." *Journal of the American Planning Association* 68, no. 2 (spring): 194–208.

New York, City of. 2001. *The Impact of the September 11 WTC Attack on NYC's Economy and City Revenues (Preliminary Estimate)*. [Accessed January 10, 2005]. Available at www.comptroller.nyc.gov/bureaus/bud/reports/WTC_Attack_Oct_4-final.pdf.

Nonprofit Risk Management Center. 2004. [Accessed January 10, 2005]. Available at www.nonprofitrisk.org/about/about.htm.

1000 Friends of Maryland and Chesapeake Bay Foundation. 1999. *Making Smart Growth Smarter: Maryland's Next Steps*. [Accessed January 10, 2005]. Available at www.cbf.org/site/PageServer?pagename=gmla_report_gmla_index.

Orfield, Myron, Jr. 1996. "Tax-Base Sharing to Reduce Fiscal Disparities." *Modernizing State Planning Statues: The Growing Smart Working Papers*, vol. 1. Planning Activity Service Report Nos. 462/463. Chicago: American Planning Association.

Organization for Economic Cooperation and Development (OECD). 2003. *Lessons Learned in Dealing with Large-Scale Disasters*. Report prepared by General Secretariat, Advisory Unit on Multi-Disciplinary Issues. SG/AU(2003)1, September 15, 2003. [Accessed January 10, 2005]. Available at www.oecd.org/dataoecd/48/39/21121542.pdf.

Palm Beach County, Florida. 2003. *Future Land-Use Element*. 1989 Comprehensive Plan, Ordinances 2002–52, 79–84. Revised February 19, 2003.

Pima County. 2004. *Sonoran Desert Conservation Plan*. [Accessed January 10, 2005]. Available at www.co.pima.az.us/cmo/sdcp/index.html.

Portland Metro. 2004. [Accessed January 10, 2005]. Available at www.metro-region.org.

Public Agency Risk Management Association (PARMA). 2004. [Accessed January 10, 2005]. Available at www.parma.com.

Public Entity Risk Institute (PERI). 2004. [Accessed January 10, 2005]. Available at www.riskinstitute.org.

Public Risk and Insurance Management Association (PRIMA). 2004. [Accessed January 10, 2005]. Available at www.primacentral.org.

Reiss, Claire Lee. 2001. *Risk Identification and Analysis: A Guide for Small Public Entities*. Fairfax, Va.: Public Entity Risk Institute.

Risk and Insurance Management Society (RIMS). 2004. [Accessed January 10, 2005]. Available at www.rims.org.

Risk Management Solutions. 2001. *World Trade Center Disaster*. Newark, Calif.: Risk Management Solutions.

_____. 2004. [Accessed January 10, 2005]. Available at www.rms.com.

Said, Carolyn. 2002. "Sept. 11 Will Cost Nation 1.64 Million Jobs, Study Says." *San Francisco Chronicle*, January 11, B1.

Schwab, Jim, Kenneth C. Topping, Charles C. Eadie, Robert E. Deyle, and Richard A. Smith. 1998. *Planning for Post-Disaster Recovery and Reconstruction*. Planning Advisory Service Report No. 483/484. Chicago: American Planning Association.

Seasons, Mark. 2003. "Monitoring and Evaluation in Municipal Planning: Considering the Realities." *Journal of the American Planning Association* 69, no. 4 (autumn): 430–440.

Simon, Roger. 2001. "Blown Away." *U.S. News & World Report, Special Report*, September 14, 16.

Smutniak, John. 2004. "Living Dangerously." *The Economist*, January 24, 3–4.

So, Frank, ed. 1979. *The Practice of Local Government Planning*. Washington D.C. International City Management Association.

Spier, Cameron, and Kurt Stephenson. 2002. "Does Sprawl Cost Us All? Isolating the Effects of Housing Patterns on Public Water and Sewer Costs." *Journal of the American Planning Association*, 68, no. 1 (winter): 56–70.

Srinivasan, Deepa. 2003. "Battling Hazards with a Brand New Tool." *Planning*, February, 10–13.

Steinburg, Michele, and Raymond J. Burby. 2002. "Growing Safe." *Planning*, April, 22–23.

Toland, Bill. 2004. "A Blueprint for Tax Sharing: In Minnesota, Dividing the Spoils Helps Cities and Suburbs." *Pittsburgh Post-Gazette*, February 15. [Accessed January 10, 2005]. Available at www.post-gazette.com/pg/04046/273339.stm.

United States Census Bureau. 2001. *Population Change and Distribution: 1990 to 2000. Census 2000 Brief*. Washington, D.C.: U.S. Department of Commerce.

United States Conference of Mayors. 2001. "Cities Face Increased Security Costs Following September 11 Attack." [Accessed January 10, 2005]. Available at www. usmayors.org/uscm/news/press_releases/documents/surveyresults_102201.asp.

United States Congressional Budget Office. 2002. Letter to the Honorable John M. Spratt Jr., Ranking Democratic Member, Committee on the Budget, U.S. House of Representatives, dated August 29, 2002. [Accessed January 10, 2005]. Available at www.cbo.gov/showdoc.cfm?index=3748&sequence=0.

United States Geological Survey (USGS). 2003. *2003 Earthquake Probability Study*. [Accessed January 10, 2005]. Available at http:quake.wr.usgs.gov/research/seismology/wg02/.

Vorderbrueggen, Lisa. 2004. "BART Aims to Seal a Deal." *Contra Costa Times*, April 17, A1.

RECENT PLANNING ADVISORY SERVICE REPORTS

Making Great Communities Happen

The American Planning Association provides leadership in the development of vital communities by advocating excellence in community planning, promoting education and citizen empowerment, and providing the tools and support necessary to effect positive change.

477. Transportation Demand Management. Erik Ferguson. March 1998. 68pp.

478. Manufactured Housing: Regulation, Design Innovations, and Development Options. Welford Sanders. July 1998. 120pp.

479. The Principles of Smart Development. September 1998. 113pp.

480/481. Modernizing State Planning Statutes: The Growing Smart^{SM} Working Papers. Volume 2. September 1998. 269pp.

482. Planning and Zoning for Concentrated Animal Feeding Operations. Jim Schwab. December 1998. 44pp.

483/484. Planning for Post-Disaster Recovery and Reconstruction. Jim Schwab, et al. December 1998. 346pp.

485. Traffic Sheds, Rural Highway Capacity, and Growth Management. Lane Kendig with Stephen Tocknell. March 1999. 24pp.

486. Youth Participation in Community Planning. Ramona Mullahey, Yve Susskind, and Barry Checkoway. June 1999. 70pp.

489/490. Aesthetics, Community Character, and the Law. Christopher J. Duerksen and R. Matthew Goebel. December 1999. 154pp.

493. Transportation Impact Fees and Excise Taxes: A Survey of 16 Jurisdictions. Connie Cooper. July 2000. 62pp.

494. Incentive Zoning: Meeting Urban Design and Affordable Housing Objectives. Marya Morris. September 2000. 64pp.

495/496. Everything You Always Wanted To Know About Regulating Sex Businesses. Eric Damian Kelly and Connie Cooper. December 2000. 168pp.

497/498. Parks, Recreation, and Open Spaces: An Agenda for the 21st Century. Alexander Garvin. December 2000. 72pp.

499. Regulating Home-Based Businesses in the Twenty-First Century. Charles Wunder. December 2000. 37pp.

500/501. Lights, Camera, Community Video. Cabot Orton, Keith Spiegel, and Eddie Gale. April 2001. 76pp.

502. Parks and Economic Development. John L. Crompton. November 2001. 74pp.

503/504. Saving Face: How Corporate Franchise Design Can Respect Community Identity (revised edition). Ronald Lee Fleming. February 2002. 118pp.

505. Telecom Hotels: A Planners Guide. Jennifer Evans-Crowley. March 2002. 31pp.

506/507. Old Cities/Green Cities: Communities Transform Unmanaged Land. J. Blaine Bonham, Jr., Gerri Spilka, and Darl Rastorfer. March 2002. 123pp.

508. Performance Guarantees for Government Permit Granting Authorities. Wayne Feiden and Raymond Burby. July 2002. 80pp.

509. Street Vending: A Survey of Ideas and Lessons for Planners. Jennifer Ball. August 2002. 44pp.

510/511. Parking Standards. Edited by Michael Davidson and Fay Dolnick. November 2002. 181pp.

512. Smart Growth Audits. Jerry Weitz and Leora Susan Waldner. November 2002. 56pp.

513/514. Regional Approaches to Affordable Housing. Stuart Meck, Rebecca Retzlaff, and James Schwab. February 2003. 271pp.

515. Planning for Street Connectivity: Getting from Here to There. Susan Handy, Robert G. Paterson, and Kent Butler. May 2003. 95pp.

516. Jobs-Housing Balance. Jerry Weitz. November 2003. 41pp.

517. Community Indicators. Rhonda Phillips. December 2003. 46pp.

518/519. Ecological Riverfront Design. Betsy Otto, Kathleen McCormick, and Michael Leccese. March 2004. 177pp.

520. Urban Containment in the United States. Arthur C. Nelson and Casey J. Dawkins. March 2004. 130pp.

521/522. A Planners Dictionary. Edited by Michael Davidson and Fay Dolnick. April 2004. 460pp.

523/524. Crossroads, Hamlet, Village, Town (revised edition). Randall Arendt. April 2004. 142pp.

525. E-Government. Jennifer Evans–Cowley and Maria Manta Conroy. May 2004. 41pp.

526. Codifying New Urbanism. Congress for the New Urbanism. May 2004. 97pp.

527. Street Graphics and the Law. Daniel Mandelker with Andrew Bertucci and William Ewald. August 2004. 133pp.

528. Too Big, Boring, or Ugly: Planning and Design Tools to Combat Monotony, the Too-big House, and Teardowns. Lane Kendig. December 2004. 103pp.

529/530. Planning for Wildfires. James Schwab and Stuart Meck. February 2005. 126pp.

531. Planning for the Unexpected: Land-Use development and Risk. Laurie Johnson, Laura Dwelley samant, and Suzanne Frew. February 2005. 59pp.

For price information, please go to www.planning.org or call 312-431-9100 and ask for the Planners Book Service. The web site also contains a complete subject and chronological index to the PAS Report series.